Praise for *Th*

"In this book R P Stevens maste
wealth in a simple, yet powerful r
J L Collins,

"For many, investing is both complex and intimidating.
Investor, through his 5 bedrock principles and naturally inactive
demeanour, provides a clear, evidence based approach to investing. It's
the perfect antidote to the complicated jargon commonly used by the
financial media."

Daniel Crosby, Author of *The Behavioral Investor*

"I really like the idea of investing slowly, patiently and persistently, with
low costs and an unshakeable focus on the long term."

William Green, Author of *Richer, Wiser, Happier*

"Investors have an in-built bias towards action, which the media only
encourages and the industry loves to exploit. But R P Stevens is perfectly
right: lethargy and sloth produce much better investor outcomes."

Robin Powell, Author of *Invest Your Way to Financial Freedom*

"Buy and hold, aka 'investing like a sloth' beats active investing for the
majority of the time."

Kristy Shen & Bryce Leung, Authors of *Quit Like a Millionaire*

"If one lesson stands out from the annals of financial history, it is that
investors get in their own way. These self-imposed hurdles often stem
from over-complicating investment strategies and/or trading too much.
For most investors, a simple investment approach is the best tactic. There
is truth to the old adage that the best performing brokerage accounts
belong to those that have died, and could no longer get in their own way.
Of the 5 'Sloth investing' principles, I think the power of simplicity is
particularly crucial."

Jamie Catherwood, Financial Historian

The Sloth Investor

R P Stevens

Troubador Publishing Ltd
Unit E2 Airfield Business Park,
Harrison Road, Market Harborough,
Leicestershire. LE16 7UL
Tel: 0116 2792299
Email: books@troubador.co.uk
Web: www.troubador.co.uk

ISBN 978 1805142 669

British Library Cataloguing in Publication Data.
A catalogue record for this book is available from the British Library.

Printed and bound by CPI Group (UK) Ltd, Croydon, CR0 4YY
Typeset in 11pt Adobe Garamond Pro by Troubador Publishing Ltd, Leicester, UK

To Justine, Leo and Keira.

Contents

Introducing the 'Sloth Investor': Lights, Camera... Inaction

Think carefully about the following statement:

Inactivity > Activity

How many realms of life does it apply to? Naturally, we're taught from a young age that it is exertion – i.e. frequent activity – that will enable us to grow and develop, and realise our full potential as human beings.

What Society Teaches Us

Outliers, a book by Malcolm Gladwell, popularised the notion that it takes 10,000 hours of intensive practice to achieve mastery of complex skills.[1] As I type these words, I sit and ponder upon notable figures, past and present, that I have admired. John Lennon and Bruce Lee, born within just seven weeks of each other, obtained mastery in their chosen disciplines. How? You guessed it: through hours and hours of exertion, of frequent activity.

---

1   Gladwell, Malcolm, *Outliers: The Story of Success* (Penguin, 2009).

Lennon, of course, was mentioned in Gladwell's book, along with his bandmates. As Gladwell was right to point out, the innumerable hours of performance that the Beatles undertook in Hamburg, Germany in their formative years laid the foundation for the global phenomenon that they would later become.

On a similar note, visiting the 'Bruce Lee Training' website[2] will allow you to learn more about the countless hours of sacrifice that it took for Bruce Lee to develop into the world-renowned martial artist that he became. These daily training routines and rigorous workouts produced, without question, the most famous martial artist of all time.

Finally, as I type these words in the wintry months of 2021, I can't help but reflect on the release of the movie *King Richard*, starring Will Smith, which explores the inspirational story of the Williams sisters' rise to tennis superstardom and the formative role that their father played in their success. During the movie, you can't help but appreciate the importance of the many hours of practice that both girls undertook to grow into the elite tennis players that they became. This is what Serena Williams said about this rigorous training regime:

"Well, they say, like, a hundred thousand hours to do it right. So definitely, definitely put in a ton of hours. Maybe it was 10,000 hours, that makes more sense… Yeah, when I was younger, I trained a lot. I used to train from eight to eleven and then one to five. That was only in the summer because I did go to school, so those were my summer hours

---

2   See: [bruceleetraining.com].

and those were very, very, very intense. I never forgot those hours."[3]

A Deadly Sin No More!

At this stage, you could be forgiven for thinking that you've picked up the wrong book. After all, isn't this supposed to be a book about investing? Well, yes it is. However, it's critically important that you recognise that the domain of investing is unique in that you will generally be rewarded more with *less* action and the *less* effort that you take.

That's right, it's time to cast away any prior fears that you held about the concept of sloth, due to its status as one of the deadly sins. Warren Buffett, undoubtedly the world's most famous investor, made an astute observation about the virtuous quality of sloth to one's investment portfolio when he made the following statement in his 1990 letter to shareholders:

> "Lethargy bordering on sloth remains the cornerstone of our investment style."

It sounds counter-intuitive, doesn't it? This lack of effort. Incidentally, you'll learn more about Buffett later in this book but, suffice to say for now, Buffett's statement played a key role in the formation of the sloth investor and his approach to investing.

---

3   "'A Hundred Thousand Hours": Serena Williams Reveals Inspiring Practice Sessions During Summer Break' by Melroy Fernandes. Published by *Essentially Sports* on 7th August 2021 – [essentiallysports. com/wta-tennis-news-a-hundred-thousand-hours-serena-williams-reveals-inspiring-practice-sessions-during-summer-break/].

Mr Bull and Mr Bear – a Polite Request: Could You Please Step Aside?

Let us now reflect for a brief moment on the humble sloth, an animal that's native to south and central America, and widely known for its slow movement and inactive lifestyle.

Despite the fact that it is the bull and the bear that has traditionally held sway over investors' imaginations, I will argue throughout this book that it is an entirely different animal, the humble sloth, that can provide us with an altogether more useful way of thinking about the world of investing.

Why is the statement 'Inactivity > Activity' so central to the book that you are currently reading? Why is a sloth the most appropriate animal to characterise successful investing?

Well, a key takeaway that I want readers of this book to have is that within the realm of investing, inactivity *outperforms* activity.

That's right, Mr Bull and Mr Bear, it's time to step aside and finally allow Mr Sloth to take his rightful place as the behavioural template for successful investing.

Life Lessons

Learn to read, learn to write, learn to swim, learn to ride a bike. These are considered to be rites of passage in a person's life, wouldn't you think?

I eventually learned to ride a bike at a relatively late age, much later than my close circle of friends at the time. Why did it take me so long to acquire the skills necessary to ride a bike? To answer that question requires me to honestly look back and assess my attitude as an eight-year-old. The recipient of a bike on Christmas Day morning, I stepped out into my garden with my father ready to assume mastery of my new two-wheeler. Except, unfortunately, that's not how things turned out. A fall, and then another fall, followed by a steadfast inability to persevere led to me throwing the bicycle on the ground, much to my father's dismay.

The Importance of a 'Can-Do' Attitude

The following day witnessed a repeat of the previous day's events. What caused my inadequacy? A lack of effort from my father? Was the bicycle too big? No, none of these reasons. The chief cause was my attitude. The phrase 'I can't do it' was repeatedly uttered to my father during those frustrating initial attempts and would continue to be uttered to friends and family members when the subject of a bike ride cropped up from time to time.

Periodically, my parents would ask whether I would like to try again, to once again attempt to obtain mastery of a bicycle – a rite of passage that comes so easily to most young people. 'I don't know how!' was the frustrated response that I commonly gave.

Why am I retelling this series of events? What do they have to do with investing?

Well, I believe there are tremendous parallels that can be drawn between my attitude towards cycling as a child and the attitudes that many people possess towards investing. Let's revisit the two phrases that I remember uttering: 'I can't do it' and 'I don't know how'.

I would argue that these two phrases are indicative of a mindset that also prevents many individuals from investing.

Invisible Scripts

Let's take the first phrase, 'I can't do it'. To many, investing seems like an alien concept, a blurry haze of difficulty that cannot be overcome. Quite simply, some people fear that they are not clever enough, that they are incapable of comprehending the world of investment. It's almost as if, for some, there is a set of invisible scripts at work, functioning to reduce the potential that they have within themselves.

A Rite of Passage

For far too many, the notion of investing gets dropped in a box marked 'too difficult' and worryingly this means that a significant number of people do nothing about growing their hard-earned money. The opportunity cost is enormous.

I firmly believe that learning how to invest money should be considered an essential rite of passage for people of all ages, but especially those of a young age, who can particularly reap the rewards of compound interest (more about compound interest a little later).

Shouldn't I Leave It to the Professionals?

Many will take the view that 'It's better to leave it to a professional'. After all, you may reflect on your capabilities and decide that you don't know enough about how to invest, or that it's too complex. However, as I will elaborate upon, the tendency for many to adopt this view is worrying due to the high cost of fees you are likely to incur when you begin to engage with the so-called 'professionals'. Moreover, a key concern for anyone looking to rely upon a 'professional' is whether they really possess the degree of expertise and insight necessary to grow your money over a sustained period of time. I will discuss this in more detail later, within the bedrock principle of 'Low Fees'.

A further hurdle for many people to overcome may be the fact that there is little or no prior history of anyone else in their family investing. One cannot overestimate the importance of the knowledge that can be acquired from informed family members, with some degree of knowledge about investing.

It Takes Too Much Time

Another barrier that can prohibit entry into the realm of investing is the perceived time it is considered to exact on one's time. For example, what to buy? What process to adopt? Work, leisure time, time with family – what time is left to commit to investing?

Fortunately for you, the simple, clear investing approach that I will advocate in this book will not require significant amounts of your time. This is the principal reason why this book is entitled *The Sloth Investor*. I have two young children and a wife, enjoy playing sports and am a voracious reader. I don't want to spend any more time on my investing portfolio than is truly necessary. Being a 'sloth investor' should appeal to your lazy gene (if, like me, you possess one).

It's Too Nerve-Racking

Finally, the perceived sense of volatility associated with the stock market deters many potential investors. However, as I will explain later on, the psychological discomfort that accompanies this volatility is the price you pay for the higher returns that the stock market offers, compared to all other forms of investment.

Of course, I completely understand the reasons that I have outlined above as these were the very same reasons that explain why I was initially reluctant to invest. As a young man, the concept of investing seemed alien to me. This isn't what someone like me, Mr Joe Average, with no background in finance, with no family history of investing, is supposed to do.

My limited awareness of the field of investing came from intermittent television news reports of the stock market. Invariably, these reports would feature a scene from the floor of the New York Stock Exchange (NYSE). The frenzied looks within the exchange room floor and the frantically moving, brightly coloured digits only served to mystify my mind, further cementing my bewildered view of what I considered to be the heady, off-limits world of investing. Yes, I was certainly a victim of imposter syndrome or, rather, investing imposter syndrome.

An Investment Approach Endorsed by Investing Giants

So, the purpose of this book is to provide individuals that have little or no experience of investing, with the knowledge that they need to invest in a rational way that is aligned with academic evidence. The approach to investing that is advocated throughout this book is endorsed by Nobel Prize winners in Economics and investing icons such as Warren Buffett and John C Bogle.

Get Your Money Moving!

I want the readers of this book to feel empowered and confident in the belief that they can be successful investors. Let's reflect again upon my references to learning to ride a bike and how to swim. It's during our formative years that we are expected to acquire the skills necessary to read and to write, to swim and to ride a bike.

Let's zero in on the latter two. Swimming and cycling are great ways to get yourself moving. I would argue that investing is also an incredibly powerful way to get your money moving in the right direction. Though it may seem harsh, the failure of some people to master the skills of swimming and cycling could result in them being cast in an odd light or considered a relative oddity. I'll go a step further and state that I find it odd that someone would not want to learn how to grow their money. As I discuss in a later chapter, there are numerous reasons why it is important to grow one's money.

Thanks to technology and the resultant democratisation of information, we are now fortunate to be living within a thin slice of history during which our understanding of how we can invest in a clear, evidence-based way has increased significantly. To some, the notion of investing is similar to joining a gym or eating more healthily. It seems like a good idea, but perhaps you've never got round to it. This book will fix that problem.

Save Your Money, Son!

"Save your money, son!" This was the message that my mother implored me to understand from a young age. It has become customary for many children to earn what the Spanish refer to as 'paga'. The Americans use the term 'allowance' and as a young Brit, I earned 'pocket money'. "Spend a little, son, but be sure to save some of your money," are invariably the words that my mum would utter. The reiteration of this point was made on numerous occasions and, indeed, it conspired to create a reflexive action on my part. The literal, physical partitioning of a select number of coins into my savings box became a weekend ritual.

Looking back, I didn't appreciate how easy my mother made this task by providing me with coins instead of a crisp £5 note. Yes, £5 was the going rate back then for the satisfactory completion of menial tasks such as tidying my room and making my mother and father occasional cups of tea and coffee. Five gleaming coins (aren't coins always gleaming to a nine-year-old?) enabled me to allocate a specific amount to my savings box each weekend. Some weeks, several coins would be placed in this hallowed box, other weeks, perhaps because I had become seduced by a comic book in a local shop, I remember only dropping one solitary coin into the box. Nonetheless, an amount, whether it be one, two or three coins, was always syphoned off into savings.

Becoming Investment Literate

So, is this a book about saving money? Well, it is and it isn't. Let me explain. Saving money is undoubtedly important to your success as an investor. It represents the fuel that will ignite your journey as an investor. In other words, it will provide the foundation for your investing success. After all, if you haven't saved any money, how are you supposed to invest?

Societal recognition of the necessity of saving money to one's own financial wellbeing has now become commonplace. As I started writing this chapter, I performed an internet search by typing the phrase 'saving money'. I received 5,860,000,000 results in response. Entering the same phrase into the books section of Amazon.co.uk elicited a return of 8,000 entries. There are truly innumerable ways that we can acquire 'savings literacy'.

However, it is my belief that society now needs to develop a greater degree of 'investment literacy'. Yes, of course it is important to save your money, but, rather than simply stating: 'Save your money!', what's the next stage? What do you do with this saved money? Unfortunately, in maths classes, or any other curricular classes, schools do not provide coverage of how to invest money. This never ceases to shock and annoy this author as considerable financial benefit can be accrued from the ability of individuals to understand and subsequently apply sound, evidence-based investing principles.

The 'Making Your Money Work for You' Puzzle

Therefore, investment literacy is undoubtedly the missing piece in the 'making your money work for you' puzzle. I believe that many people are undernourished in this regard. Indeed, if you forgive my somewhat crass terminology, I would argue that there is a bewildered herd, representing great swathes of the global population, that are woefully ignorant of how to invest their money in a rational, evidence-based manner.

For example, in reference to my home country of the UK, there is a lack of emphasis assigned to investment literacy in the British educational system. Could it be that the UK government expects individuals to acquire this information through a form of magic or divine intervention?

Please forgive my facetiousness but I believe it is about time that this sorry state of affairs is swept away with the debris of history. Therefore, a chief aim of *The Sloth Investor* is to function as a corrective to the problem of investment illiteracy in both the UK and around the world. At this stage, I'll plonk my sloth investor flag in the sand and boldly declare that my mission is to 'simplify investing for all'.

Climb into the Intersection

If we were to take a look at a Venn diagram with one circle labelled 'Skilled Saver' and one circle labelled 'Skilled Investor', my goal is to ensure that my readers feel confident in placing themselves within the intersection of this Venn diagram. After reading this book, I want you to have the confidence to state that you have developed the knowledge and understanding necessary to become not only a skilled saver, but a skilled investor, too. Are you ready to climb into the intersection?

What's Ahead?

As we've already noted, the two animals most commonly associated with the stock market are the bull and the bear. In Chapter 1, I take a deeper dive into why I consider the humble, slow-moving sloth to be the most suitable animal to characterise the world of investing.

As I've already noted, I believe that one factor that deters a significant number of people from investing is the presence of 'imposter syndrome'. Therefore, the rationale of Chapter 2 is to enable you to understand how three ordinary people (a mechanic, a teacher and a secretary) were able to become extraordinary investors.

In Chapter 3, I'll introduce you to a roll call of investing luminaries. They represent FIFI, my carefully assembled team of Five International Fantasy Investors. Each member of this team of investing legends will provide you with a series of sage lessons about how to invest your money.

Chapter 4 begins with an examination of the reasons why you should invest. This then leads on to a subsection of the chapter, which digs down into what the stock market is, with an introduction to key investment vocabulary and a focus on the reasons why a company's share price may increase or decrease. The chapter closes with an exploration of the different types of investments available to you.

I consider Chapter 5 to be the most important section of the book. This is because it will provide you with the foundation for the sloth-like approach to investing that I advocate throughout this book. The rationale for these principles stems from the lessons I have learned from the investing legends discussed in Chapter 3. Indeed, to go even further, it is the knowledge that I have distilled from these individuals, allied with the investment wisdom of the three ordinary individuals discussed in Chapter 2, that will provide you with an actionable road map to become a sloth investor yourself.

In Chapter 6, you'll learn more about other important elements for your consideration as an investor. For example, I discuss the role that bonds can perform in your portfolio.

Chapter 7 outlines the rise of Vanguard, the company founded by the late Jack Bogle, a leading provider of index funds, and a key influence on my investment philosophy. As the chapter progresses, I provide a distinction between two ways that individuals invest their hard-earned money using Vanguard's products. These are 'Off the Shelf' and 'Do-it-yourself' (DIY).

Chapter 8 really gets into the nuts and bolts of *how* one can invest like a sloth. I've read numerous investment books myself, many of which I've enjoyed tremendously. However, my critique of some of them is that while rich on theory, they're lacking in utility – i.e. specificity. Therefore, I've sought to ensure that this investment book represents a union of theory and utility. This explains the clarity that I've aimed for in Chapter 8. In the chapter, I provide readers from around the globe with a choice of specific funds that they can put to work (in a sloth-like manner, of course).

Chapter 9 presents a series of real-life sloth investors for the reader to learn from. These individuals share why and how they invest and the advice they would give other investors.

While Chapters 2, 3 and 9 provide you with models for investment success, the core aim of Chapter 10 is to provide you with a series of investors that you certainly shouldn't seek to emulate. The chapter provides examples of common mistakes that people make when investing.

It is my sincere hope that this book can help to demystify the process of investing. I firmly believe that a careful reading of Chapters 1 to 10 will provide the reader with a solid understanding of how they can get their sloth investment journey started.

However, it is inevitable that some readers may still possess some lingering questions. Therefore, in the absence of a crystal ball, I have done my best to anticipate what these questions may be and you will see these questions and the accompanying answers in the final chapter of the book.

Mr Sloth's Summary:

- Inactivity outperforms activity within the realm of investing.
- Saving money is important, but it will only take you so far. Investing your savings enables your money tree to become well watered and to grow each year. It's truly remarkable how a few initial seeds can allow your money tree to blossom into something truly remarkable.

A Trip to the Zoo

"Lethargy bordering on sloth remains the cornerstone of our investment style."

Warren Buffett,
Berkshire Hathaway's 1990 letter to shareholders

"An investment strategy inspired by sloth runs circles around most professionally managed portfolios."

Andrew Hallam, *Millionaire Expat*

Step Aside, Bull and Bear!

How many investment-themed books feature a trip to the zoo? This book does, as I believe that several of the creatures within the animal kingdom provide us with important lessons that can be applied to the world of investing. Of course, the two animals most commonly associated with the stock market are the bull and the bear.

The term 'bull market' is used to describe a stock market that is rising, with increasing prices. Conversely, the term 'bear market' is used to describe a declining stock market, with prices that are decreasing.

However, I will argue throughout this book that it is an entirely different animal, the sloth, that can provide us with a more useful way of thinking about the realm of investing.

The Meerkat

Once upon a time, a boy and his father visited the zoo. The father was keen to share his love of the animal kingdom with the boy and he delighted in observing the wonderment that his son took from encountering several new animals for the first time. Naturally, though, some animals intrigued the boy more than others. For example, he was ceaselessly fascinated by the animated, knee-jerk movements of the meerkat. The boy's eyes grew wide as he took in each anxious movement of the meerkat's body.

The Uneventful Sloth

Later that day, they visited an enclosure containing a sloth. The boy's behavioural response to the sloth contrasted significantly with the delight that he had previously taken in the meerkat. While the rapid movements of the meerkat entertained and delighted the boy, the slow, sluggish behaviour of the sloth made little impression. It wasn't long before the boy was heard to state: "Dad, this animal is boring, can we go back and see the meerkats?" There was still time to spare and the boy's father had also enjoyed his time observing the meerkats – the same small carnivoran animals that had engendered such affection in his son. "Sure," said the boy's father. *It's understandable*, he thought. After all, the sloth's inactivity was no match for the rapid, animated movements of the meerkats on display.

The father and son I have described are, of course, my son and myself. Looking back, it is easy to understand how the high-energy movement of the meerkat captured my son's attention. The sloth, in comparison, stood little chance. The sloth moves more slowly than any other mammal on earth. An animal defined by such distinct inactivity generally receives little mention in the public sphere. Despite watching numerous nature documentaries through the years, I can recall just one documentary that featured this humble, slow-moving mammal.

The Most Appropriate Animal to Characterise Successful Investing

It is at this point, though, that any unfavourable references to the sloth will stop. Indeed, I will argue throughout this book that the characteristics displayed by the sloth are the very same characteristics that an investor should aspire to. As I will outline repeatedly, a careful study of the slow-moving, inactive traits of the sloth provides an investor with the necessary modus operandi for investing success.

Let's not forget the meerkat, though. This creature was the recipient of my son's affection that sunny afternoon in the zoo. In addition, I've lost count of the innumerable occasions that I've witnessed the exploits of this creature on my television screen in the UK, on nature documentaries and within myriad advertising campaigns. The animated, playful movements of the meerkat certainly elicit great affection and attention from onlookers. However, the differences between the meerkat and the sloth can help us to understand why some people succeed as investors, while others struggle. Observing the meerkat closely, we can see that it is constantly 'on edge', unable to relax. I believe that the twitchy, anxiety-laden demeanour of the meerkat provides the closest approximation to the unfortunate behaviour that is demonstrated by many investors today. I use the term 'unfortunate' to describe this behaviour because the adoption of such a mentality in investors is a certain recipe for investing distress.

A Behavioural Template for Successful Investing

The sloth on the other hand provides us with the best behavioural template and the most appropriate mental model for our success as investors. 'Less is more' and 'hands off' are also terms we could use to describe the sloth-like approach to investing that I will advocate throughout this book. Despite the evidence in favour of a sloth-like approach to investing, you are unlikely to read about such a philosophy in much of the financial media.

This is a shame because it's the approach to investing that has been recommended by Nobel Prize-winning economists and investing giants such as Warren Buffett. Indeed, in 2004, Google invited three advocates of this approach to investing to speak to their employees.[4] These individuals were William F Sharpe, a Nobel Prize winner;

---

4   [ritholtz.com/2006/12/the-best-investment-advice-youll-never-get]
     – retrieved December 29th, 2021.

Burton Malkiel, a Princeton economics professor; and John Bogle, the man who revolutionised investing for the ordinary, everyday retail investor.

Google recognised that many of their employees were about to become very rich, but were also aware that many of them could fall prey to the predatory financial sharks that invariably feast upon high-net-worth individuals. All of the experts provided the same advice to Google employees. Build portfolios of low-cost index funds. This simple, sloth-like approach to investing is what you will learn about in this book.

Mr Sloth's Summary:

- The bull and the bear are the two animals most commonly associated with the stock market. However, it is the humble sloth that provides the most appropriate mental model for successful investing.

Once Upon a Time…

Once upon a time, there were three ordinary individuals who became extraordinary investors. A teacher, a mechanic and a secretary.

Reflecting upon their stories has positively affected me and how I invest. This is because each of their lives taught me, and can teach you, important lessons about the world of investing. Indeed, these lessons help to form the foundation for the sloth-like approach to investing that I endorse and elaborate upon in this book.

Andrew Hallam – the Millionaire Teacher

Expatriate teachers owe a tremendous amount of gratitude to Andrew Hallam. Working internationally certainly brings great benefits. The opportunity to travel, meet people from around the world and vastly broaden one's professional expertise are some of the key positives of working internationally.

Perhaps most significantly for some, the opportunity to earn a higher salary and the prospect of subsidised, often free, housing (this is dependent on location) compels many to leave their country of origin. Hence, it is commonly the case that the 'package' offered to an expatriate teacher (as Andrew Hallam once was) will tip the scales in favour of a prolonged career abroad. Reflecting upon the advantages of teaching abroad, one could be tempted to state that it is a 'no-brainer' decision for teaching professionals. While I would agree with this to a strong extent, one should recognise that one of the disadvantages of a teaching career abroad is that it is commonly the case that teachers will not automatically be able to contribute towards a professional pension scheme, such as would have been the case if they had remained in their home country's teaching system. This, obviously, creates a problem.

Enter Andrew Hallam, one of Canada's finest exports. Andrew's first book was called *Millionaire Teacher* because, you guessed it, Andrew became a millionaire teacher. Andrew has written several books on investing. His book, *Millionaire Expat: How to Build Wealth Living Overseas*, has been of great benefit to innumerable expats.

Andrew's books have been a godsend to expatriate teachers and, indeed, non-teaching expatriates, because he clearly sets out the principles of common-sense, simple, smart investing. These are, of course, the very same principles that enabled him to become a millionaire teacher. So, I hear you cry, what are these principles? Spill the proverbial beans. Don't worry, the aim of this book is to drill down into the investing philosophy that Andrew and many other common-sense, rational-thinking investors have written about.

The Millionaire Mechanic

At this stage, what I want to do is to provide a little background concerning how Andrew acquired his solid, practical investing philosophy. In 2018, Andrew sat down to conduct an interview with Caroline Leon and Keith O'Malley Farrell (hosts of *A Life of Education* podcast) to discuss his investing philosophy and background.[5] In one fascinating section of the interview, Andrew revealed that he developed an understanding of how to invest by talking to a millionaire mechanic named Russ Perry while working at a bus maintenance garage on a temporary basis.

Yes, you read that correctly, a millionaire mechanic. In the interview, Andrew recalled how his fellow workers at the garage stated that: "There's a mechanic here who's a millionaire." Andrew's response, purely understandable, was: "Nah, that's impossible." Andrew recalled that his fellow workers then informed him that the mechanic was forty-seven years old, had two children and to reiterate again that he was a millionaire.

In what I consider to be the key moment in the retelling, Andrew's co-workers, as recalled by Andrew, state that: "If he ever talks to you about money, you listen." Now, at this point, Andrew had a binary set of choices. Disregard what his fellow co-workers were telling him or listen to what the millionaire mechanic had to say about money. Wisely, he chose the latter option, and the smart

---

5   Leon, C, *A Life of Education* podcast. Episode 24: 'Millionaire Ex-
      pat Andrew Hallam' (published on YouTube 26th October 2010)
      – [youtube.com/watch?v=nO-FbzNOjWY].

decision to do so has exerted a positive, compound effect on many people's lives.

I will refer to the magic of compound interest on many occasions throughout this book. It can take many forms. Let's reflect a little on the decision that Andrew Hallam took. He chose to listen to the millionaire mechanic and subsequently learnt from him how to invest his money in a smart, rational way. Obviously, the most immediate beneficiary was Andrew as he was the initial recipient of this information. As a young man, Andrew was able to apply the common-sense, rational approach to investing that he was fortunate enough to acquire from his millionaire mechanic co-worker. Moreover, during his time as an expat teacher, Andrew ran investing workshops at his international school. Finally, and of even more significance given their impact, he has been able to reach an even wider audience by writing several books in which he has outlined his approach towards investing.

Compound interest can take varied forms, never forget that. Money compounds, but knowledge also compounds. Personal finance workshops, a series of books, podcast interviews – the ripple effect of Andrew's decision to listen to the millionaire mechanic has undoubtedly been huge. Likewise, as a reader of this book, I sincerely hope that you are able to pass on or 'pay forward' the actionable, investing wisdom that I believe is contained within this book.

If you have the time, I encourage you to watch the podcast interview. It would be a great way to invest an hour of your time.

Grace Groner – the Millionaire Secretary

At first glance, Grace Groner does not look like your stereotypical investor. And yet, during her life, she possessed many of the essential qualities needed by a sloth investor. Let me tell you a little bit about her life.

Grace was born in 1909 in the city of Lake Forest, Illinois, forty-five minutes north of Chicago in the United States. At the age of twelve, she became an orphan after both her parents died. George Anderson, a prominent member of the community, cared for Grace and her twin sister, Gladys. She spent most of her life in a one-bedroom house and lived what appeared to be a quiet, unremarkable life.

In 1931, she accepted a position as a secretary at Abbott Laboratories, an American healthcare company. She maintained this position for forty-three years. Grace's pay as a secretary was modest and she had also lived through the Great Depression, which meant that Grace lived frugally. However, despite her instinct for frugality, Grace did not exhibit miserly tendencies. For example, she is said to have donated money anonymously in her community and travelled later in her life.

In 1935, the year that she turned twenty-six, and several years after she started working for Abbott Laboratories, she used her savings to purchase three shares of Abbott's company stock.[6] This amounted to $60 a share or $180 in total. Investing in the stock market became more common

---

6   'How a Secretary Made and Gave Away $7 Million' by Robert Frank. Published by *The Wall Street Journal* on 8th March 2010 – [wsj.com/articles/BL-WHB-2769].

for American households during and after the First World War. Charlie Chaplin, the silent movie star, appeared in front of the New York Stock Exchange in 1918. Chaplin had been asked to promote Liberty Bonds, a form of investment, to help finance American involvement in the First World War. Promotional appeals by movie stars such as Charlie Chaplin encouraged ordinary Americans to become investors. Was Grace Groner's decision to invest influenced by Chaplin? We shall never know. However, we do know that Groner's decision to invest would exert great influence upon the lives of others in the decades to come.

When Grace Groner passed away at the age of one hundred on January 19th 2010, she left $7 million, which would be used to fund the Grace Elizabeth Groner Foundation. This foundation seeks to enrich young people's education and future. The establishment of such an honourable foundation is fantastic. Naturally, though, the source of the foundation's funds may have puzzled some observers at the time. Where did Grace get all of that money? Was it inherited? Did she win the state lottery? No, it was neither of these two scenarios.

Grace simply continued to invest a partial amount of her salary at Abbott Laboratories and she then allowed time and the magic of compound interest to work its wonders on her stock portfolio. Grace understood the importance of investing her money and not trading. Of critical importance to her success was that she possessed an investor's mentality and not a trader's mentality. The former approach to investing is defined by a 'buy-and-hold' mindset. You purchase a stock position and then you hold on to it. Conversely, the latter approach, the trader's mentality, is looking to 'make a quick buck'.

The remarkable story of Grace Groner teaches us many lessons about what it takes to be a successful investor. Firstly, as an investor, Grace appeared to possess an impregnable mindset, remaining impervious to external geopolitical events and the periodic bouts of volatility that they cause. This is a crucial component to successful investing, the ability to 'turn off the noise' and remain committed to investing at all times, through good times and bad.

Let's think about some of the tumultuous times that Grace lived through during her time as an investor. In 1939, the Second World War began; in 1950, there was the Korean War; in 1962, the world could have ended with the onset of the Cuban Missile Crisis. You can imagine the jitters that these key geopolitical events would have caused in the minds of many investors and yet Grace Groner stayed true and committed to her investing journey.

I use the word 'journey' because that's what investing is. Every journey has highs and lows, and Grace's shares would inevitably have experienced both euphoric highs and depressing lows. It would have been easy for investors to pull out and to sell during the depressing lows caused by the extreme geopolitical events that occurred during the period from 1930 to 2010 (this is the period during which Grace invested).

However, Grace demonstrated the attributes of a sloth investor, in that she refused to cower to the volatility that is an inevitable feature of the life of an investor. When investing, and particularly when engaging in the form of sloth investing, inactivity outperforms activity and, to her credit, Grace Groner seemed to understand this from a young age.

Grace Groner's time horizon as an investor, her temperament and her steadfast ability to remain invested at all times provides a fantastic example of how a seemingly ordinary, average person can become an extraordinary investor.

An Injection of Nuance – What Grace Did Wrong

At this stage, I would like to state that some nuance is required when reflecting upon Grace Groner's remarkable investing story. I wholeheartedly endorse the approach for its 'buy-and-hold' flavour, i.e. Grace repeatedly purchased a stock market position and then held it through thick and thin, through good times and bad, over a very long time period. However, it is important to note that Grace solely invested in one company. This is extremely risky and something that I will certainly not advocate in this book.

Fortunately for Grace, this company's stock, the stock of her employer, performed well over a sustained period of time. However, if this company had not performed well, Grace's fortune would never have materialised. Therefore, rather than rigidly adhering to Grace's exact investing strategy, I encourage readers to take a more nuanced view of her approach.

Yes, you should certainly adhere to a long-term time horizon when investing and should also continue to invest during times of geopolitical upheaval. However, and this cannot be stressed enough, you should *never* invest in only one company. This runs counter to the importance of diversification, which I will explore in much greater detail later in the book.

Mr Sloth's Summary:

- Ordinary people can become extraordinary investors. Learning from the rational sloth-like investment decisions of other 'ordinary' people can enable you to generate extraordinary results with your investments.
- Andrew Hallam's writing has been a key influence on the investment philosophy of the Sloth Investor. You can learn more about Andrew by visiting andrewhallam. com.
- The remarkable story of Grace Groner provides sloth investors with many important lessons. She started early in life, giving her money a long time frame to grow. In addition, Grace hung on to the shares through thick and thin, not allowing her emotions to be swayed by geopolitical events or the behaviour of other investors.

Standing on the Shoulders of Giants

> "If I have seen further than others, it is by standing
> upon the shoulders of giants."
>
> Sir Isaac Newton

I'm fond of the above quote because of its relevance to the world of investing. One of my key aims in writing this book is for you, the reader, to learn from the wisdom of great investors, past and present. It is my hope that by standing on the metaphorical shoulders of these investors, you will indeed be able to see further than others, developing an investing philosophy that will enable you to avoid the pitfalls that beset so many other investors.

A Compound Creation

The author of this book is a compound creation of two groups of investors. Firstly, the three ordinary people (but ultimately, extraordinary investors) I mentioned in the previous chapter allied with the five investing titans that I will expand on during this chapter.

Moreover, the lessons I have learned from these investors have provided me with the intellectual underpinning of the five bedrock principles (**S**implicity, **L**ow Fees, **O**wning the World, **T**ime in the Market, **H**eadstrong) that form the foundation for a sloth investor's approach to investing.

Mr Sloth's Love of Language and Love of Football

Being a sloth investor enables me to spend time on leisure pursuits I enjoy. Two of the principal passions that I possess are a love of language and a love of football. I'm now going to draw upon both passions to shine more light upon the world of investing.

Firstly, as a language enthusiast, I have always been drawn to etymology – the study of words. So, where does the word 'invest' originate from? It is derived from the Latin verb *investire*, meaning 'to clothe'. As someone keen to illuminate positive figures from the world of investing, which five fantasy investors would I select to clothe in the kit of my own fantasy investing team? Let me explain a little more below.

Step Aside FIFA… Enter FIFI!

Now, on to the second of the two passions I mentioned. I enjoy both watching football and playing football. For many years, I have played five-a-side football. This shortened version of the beautiful game is fun and provides a good workout for this particular sloth investor. What connection could I draw between the world of investing and five-a-side football? Well, many football fans like to participate in something known as 'fantasy football'. For the uninitiated, this game requires the football fan to construct a fantasy team by selecting eleven players of their choice. This team then competes against other fans' fantasy teams in a season-long league system.

I started to consider the investors that would be deserving of a place on my fantasy investing team. So, without further ado, here they are: the founding members of the **F**ive **I**nternational **F**antasy **I**nvestors team or, to use the more affectionate acronym, FIFI (apologies, FIFA). Okay, so they may not score many goals on the football pitch, and their team name is unconventional and likely to evoke ridicule, but learning from their combined investing nous will definitely teach you more about the qualities needed to become a sloth investor.

Jack Bogle

Tasked with sculpting the equivalent of our own investing Mount Rushmore – a monument to honour significant giants of the investing world – my first pick would be Jack Bogle.

Not only does he take pride of place on my fictitious monument to investing, but he also simultaneously becomes the first pick for my five-a-side fantasy team. Why is this? Quite simply, the foundation for the approach to investing that I advocate throughout this book stems from Bogle's decision to create the world's first index fund in 1976.

Referring to the significance of index funds in a speech in 2005, Paul Samuelson, winner of a Nobel Prize in Economic Sciences, stated:

> "I rank this Bogle invention (the index fund) along with
> the invention of the wheel, the alphabet, Gutenberg
> printing, and wine and cheese."[7]

High praise indeed. Now, the question you are probably asking, dear reader, is: 'What is an index fund?' As I explain, I'm confident that it will become clear why Samuelson conjured parallels between Bogle's index fund creation and the wheel, the alphabet and the Gutenberg printing press.

Introducing (Clears Throat)... the Index Fund!

An index fund tracks the stock market in a passive way, buying a small amount of *everything*. Therefore, instead of trying to outdo the return of the stock market by investing in individual companies or individual market sectors, index funds provide investors with a hands-off, inactive (sloth-like) approach to investing. In his book *Trillions*, author Robin Wigglesworth states:

> "In the annals of Wall Street, the index fund is one
> of the few truly, nearly unambiguously beneficial
> inventions, a disruptive technology that has already

---

7   '*Why the world's biggest investor backs the simplest investment*' by Tim Harford. Published by BBC News on 17th July 2017 – [bbc.co.uk/news/business-40189970].

> saved investors hundreds of billions of dollars, sums that will undoubtedly reach trillions in years to come."[8]

The beauty of an index fund is that it enables individuals to invest their money in a low-cost manner while achieving magnificent results. At the time of its creation, Bogle's competitors within the field of investing dismissively referred to the notion of an index fund as 'Bogle's folly'. However, these claims did not deter Bogle for he had become accustomed in his life to overcoming adversity.

A Harsh Economic Reality for Young Jack

Jack Bogle was born in 1929 in the town of Montclair, New Jersey in the United States. Jack's family was adversely affected by the Great Depression. The family had to sell their house as a result of the harsh economic reality of the time. Moreover, Jack's father developed depression and subsequently became an alcoholic. This contributed to the divorce of his parents. As we can see, like many other American children of the time, Bogle had a turbulent start to life. Despite the challenges that he faced, Bogle joined Princeton University in 1947, studying economics and investment. In 1974, Jack Bogle founded Vanguard, an investment company that I will repeatedly refer to throughout this book.

---

8   Wigglesworth, Robin, *Trillions: How a Band of Wall Street Renegades Invented the Index Fund and Changed Finance Forever* (Penguin, 2021).

A Monumental Influence

As his place on my investing Mount Rushmore would appear to testify, Bogle's influence on the world of investing has truly been monumental. Again, it's a point worth repeating that index funds have enabled non-professional, retail investors to invest their money in an inexpensive, practical way. Warren Buffett, arguably the world's most famous investor, has been unremitting in his praise of John Bogle's influence on the man-in-the-street, individual, retail investor.

In his 2016 Berkshire Hathaway letter to shareholders, Buffett stated:

> "For decades, Jack has urged investors to invest in ultra-low-cost index funds… In his early years, Jack was frequently mocked by the investment-management industry. Today, however, he has the satisfaction of knowing that he helped millions of investors realise far better returns on their savings than they otherwise would have earned. He is a hero to them and to me."[9]

Throughout this book, I will outline how you can adopt an approach to investing that is heavily defined by a commitment to index funds, enabling you to begin your journey as a sloth investor.

---

9   Buffett, Warren, *Berkshire Hathaway Annual Letter to Shareholders 2016* (25th February 2017) – [berkshirehathaway.com/letters/2016ltr.pdf].

Numero Uno on Mr Sloth's Mount Rushmore of Investing

Jack Bogle – numero uno, the first place on my team, an investing giant and a figure truly worthy of being sculpted in stone and included on my Mount Rushmore of investing. As a true titan within the field of investing, Jack Bogle also deserves a leading role on the football field. Therefore, he is undoubtedly deserving of my team's captaincy. Jack Bogle, step forward and wear with pride the captain's armband of my fantasy investors football team – you deserve it.

Warren Buffett

Innumerable books have now been written about Warren Buffett, unquestionably the world's most famous investor. Buffett is the chairman and CEO of Berkshire Hathaway, an American multinational conglomerate holding company. Terms such as 'the Oracle' and 'the Sage of Omaha' (Berkshire Hathaway is headquartered in Omaha, Nebraska) are often used to refer to Warren Buffett. At the time of writing, he remains one of the richest people in the world. The principal reason why he merits inclusion on my team is because of his advocacy for index funds. That's right, you might think that someone with Buffett's money and impressive backroom team would recommend the application of complex mathematical formulae to buy stocks. However, you would be mistaken.

Warren's Annual Words of Wisdom

On an annual basis, Berkshire Hathaway publishes a shareholder letter, penned by Warren Buffett himself. In the 2013 shareholder letter, Buffett had this to say about stock buying:

> "The goal of the non-professional should not be to pick winners – neither he nor his 'helpers' can do that – but should rather be to own a cross-section of businesses that in aggregate are bound to do well."[10]

Later on in this book, I will explore the notion of 'advantage' – i.e. what advantage do you, the non-professional, have when investing? Buffett understands the non-advantage – i.e. the disadvantage that besets individual investors – and this is why he states that instead of trying to select 'winners', the non-professional would be better off owning an index fund. This is what he suggests when he refers to 'owning a cross-section of businesses that in aggregate are bound to do well'.

Like Buffett, Bogle and Hallam, this book will champion the use of index funds for the individual investor.

Plans for Mrs Buffett

Later on in the 2014 shareholder letter, Buffett further nails his colours to the indexing mast when he discusses plans for the trustees of his estate upon his death.

---

10   Buffett, Warren, *Berkshire Hathaway Annual Letter to Shareholders 2013* (28th February 2014) – [berkshirehathaway.com/letters/2013ltr.pdf].

> "One bequest provides that cash will be delivered to a trustee for my wife's benefit... My advice to the trustee could not be more simple: Put 10% of the cash in short-term government bonds and 90% in a very low-cost S&P 500 index fund. (I suggest Vanguard's.) I believe the trust's long-term results from this policy will be superior to those attained by most investors – whether pension funds, institutions or individuals – who employ high-fee managers."[11]

So, there you have it: common-sense, sloth-like advice for the individual investor. I encourage you to profit from the wisdom of Warren Buffett's sound financial sense. For those of you that are keen to learn more from Buffett, I encourage you to read Berkshire Hathaway's shareholder letters. These are freely available online and several books have also been written that summarise the key points from each meeting. Moreover, a quick search on YouTube will enable you to unearth a considerable wealth of interview footage containing the great man himself.

Benjamin Graham

Mentor to Warren Buffett and author of one of the seminal books on investing, there are many reasons why Benjamin Graham warrants a place on our fantasy investors team. However, the key reason why I have chosen him is because of what he teaches us about investor psychology. Many people associate the world of investing as primarily a number-

---

11   Ibid.

oriented discipline. However, as I will argue in more detail later on in this book, successful investing is contingent upon the careful control of one's own emotions.

In his book, *The Intelligent Investor*[12] – heralded by Warren Buffett as "The best book about investing ever written." – Graham utilises a fitting allegory that provides investors with a solid psychological framework that they should consider when thinking about the ups and downs of the stock market.

Mr Market

Graham introduces us to 'Mr Market', an imagined investor representing the stock market as a whole, whose investment decisions are driven by emotionality instead of sound investment sense. Mr Market is susceptible to extreme swings of pessimism and optimism. Mr Market's emotional vulnerability – what some may today term bipolar behaviour – creates wide-ranging highs and lows in stock prices. These highs and lows then compel many other investors to engage in their own form of ill-advised, irrational behaviour. What effect does this behaviour have? The effect becomes exponential; a domino effect, characterised by an extreme bout of herd-like behaviour by investors, is set in motion and this is what causes the extreme pendulum swings in stock prices that we have become historically accustomed to.

---

12 Graham, B., *The Intelligent Investor: The Definitive Book on Value Investing – A Book of Practical Counsel* (Bibliophilist Publisher Books).

Turn Off the Noise!

The crucial lesson to be learned from Benjamin Graham's parable is that instead of succumbing and being influenced by the often volatile, emotional state of Mr Market, investors should simply 'turn off the noise' and commit to investing over a long period of time. Benjamin Graham's formulation of 'Mr Market' is an appropriate lens for us to apply to the stock market as it beautifully encapsulates the reason why:

A) Many people don't even begin investing.
B) A significant number of people perform poorly when investing.

In reference to point A, many people don't begin investing because they are immediately concerned about the volatility historically associated with this form of investing. However, what these people don't recognise is that volatility is a natural component of the stock market. Volatility should not be feared because it is the price that is paid for the promise of long-term positive returns. To the latter point, point B, a significant number of people perform poorly as investors because they become too heavily influenced by the erratic behaviour of Mr Market instead of adhering to a sound set of investment principles, such as investing for a long period of time and switching off 'market noise'.

Psychology plays a profound, underappreciated role in the success of investors. Hence, for creating Mr Market, such a pertinent parable for the world of investing, Benjamin

Graham is undeniably deserving of third place on our fantasy investors football team.

Morgan Housel

Morgan Housel merits a place in my FIFI team because he is quite simply my favourite investment writer. My favourite piece of Morgan Housel's writing is 'The Psychology of Money'[13], a 9,000-word article that he published in 2018. It is one of the most compelling, insightful pieces of investment writing ever composed.

The Importance of Psychology

In the piece, Housel expands upon the key, underappreciated role that psychology plays within the arena of investing. Early on in the text, Housel states:

> "Investing is not the study of finance, it's the study of how people behave with money."[14]

Building on this point, Housel then goes on to state:

> "The finance industry talks too much about what to do, and not enough about what happens in your head when you try to do it."

---

13 'The Psychology of Money' by Morgan Housel. Published on *Collab Fund* on 1st June 2018 – [collaborativefund.com/blog/the-psychology-of-money].

14 Ibid.

Housel used to write for The Motley Fool, an American financial services company. I strongly encourage you to read the articles that he penned during his time at the company. They provide an invaluable source of investing foresight and actionable advice.

One of my favourite articles by Housel is entitled 'Tyranny of the Calendar'[15], in which he comments upon the relentless desire of investment commentators to focus upon one-year returns. This article resonated strongly with me as I truly believe that rather than focusing on one-year returns, investors should, in true sloth investor fashion, focus upon a multi-decade time horizon.

All of the articles that Morgan Housel wrote during his time at The Motley Fool can be found online.[16] In addition, Morgan Housel regularly presents at a range of functions related to the world of investing, many of which have been filmed (so a quick YouTube search of his name comes highly recommended). Time invested by you viewing one of his astute, well-crafted presentations will be time well spent.

Robin Powell

While the first four positions on my fantasy five-a-side investing team have been filled by Americans, the fifth place goes to an individual from my home country of the United Kingdom. This is certainly not a token gesture,

---

15   'Tyranny of the Calendar' by Morgan Housel. Published on The Motley Fool on 29th September 2015 – [fool.com/investing/general/2015/09/29/the-tyranny-of-the-calendar.aspx].

16   Morgan Housel on The Motley Fool – [fool.com/author/1611/]. This link contains all of the articles that Housel wrote during his time at The Motley Fool.

though. Robin Powell is a highly rated, award-winning financial journalist and a tireless advocate for index funds. This approach to investing has a much higher profile in the United States and so it is both refreshing and encouraging to take note of a British financial journalist who regularly expounds the virtues of this common-sense, sloth-like form of investing.

There are several ways that you can follow Robin Powell's sound, incisive financial writing. Firstly, Powell refers to himself as 'The Evidence-Based Investor' and his blog[17] provides a wealth of information for individual investors. In particular, Powell has produced a numerous amount of video content that is freely available on the blog. While reading this book, you may be keen to further explore the arguments for index fund investing. If this is the case, I wholly recommend that you indeed view the video section[18] of Powell's website.

Robin Powell's social media feed on X (formerly Twitter) is also an invaluable resource for British index investors. On a daily basis, he provides wisdom-laden analysis of finance-related news in both the British and international media. Moreover, his posts amplify the importance of investing in a rational, evidence-based manner. Powell recognises that financial literacy in the U.K is relatively poor. For several years, information and resources for index investors in a British context were scarce. Therefore, Robin Powell's blog, his social media feed on X and his co-written book with

---

17 See: [evidenceinvestor.com].
18 Powell, Robin. *on The Evidence-Based Investor* – [evidenceinvestor.com/video].

Ben Carlson, *Invest Your Way to Financial Freedom*, seeks to address this problem. As a ceaseless proponent for this evidence-based approach to investing, Powell should be commended for his efforts to illuminate the compelling case for index fund investing to a British audience.

Investing Exemplars

Success leaves track marks and clues, and I sincerely hope that each of these noteworthy members of FIFI has started to provide you with a deeper understanding of how you can invest your money in a sloth-like manner.

In the teaching profession, it is common – and best practice – to use exemplars to teach students. Likewise, in assembling my team of five international fantasy investors and the three 'ordinary' individuals that preceded them (highlighted in Chapter 2), my goal is for you to aspire to learn from the sage wisdom of these investing luminaries. Ultimately, I consider each of them to be a 'model' for your success as a sloth investor. These investment exemplars (or models) will help to provide you with an investing roadmap that you can begin to implement and achieve success with.

Mr Sloth's Summary:

- The sloth investor is a compound creation of all that I
  have learned about investing, not least the five members
  of FIFI – my fictional five-a-side investing super team.
  The five bedrock principles of the sloth investor –
  Simplicity, **L**ow Fees, **O**wning the World, **T**ime in the
  Market and **H**eadstrong – stem from my interpretation
  of their investing philosophy.

Replicating the sound advice of the members of FIFI
(Five International Fantasy Investors) can enable you to
become a sloth investor.

Learning More About Investing

Combat Inflation

Are you committed to saving money? If yes, then that's a great start. However, if saving money forms the cornerstone of your financial philosophy, then you're likely losing money. This is because a financial philosophy that is purely defined by the sole intention of saving money will not enable you to tackle the ugly reality of inflation. Inflation is the silent thief of the money world and you must take steps to overcome it.

A Reduction in Purchasing Power

Inflation is the rate at which the prices of goods and services in the economy are increasing, which reduces the purchasing power of your money. Inflation is a natural part of the growth of an economy. Quite simply, as the demand for goods and services increase, so do prices. A little bit of inflation is healthy, but too much inflation can rapidly diminish your standard of living. The rate of inflation will affect the 'real' interest that you receive from your bank savings account. For example, if you receive 2.5% on your bank savings account and inflation is 2.5%, then the interest rate that you have actually received on your savings is 0%.

When Saving Is Not Enough

Therefore, before you begin to give yourself a congratulatory backslap because of the amount that you have saved, you must understand that saving alone will often not be enough to beat or even keep pace with inflation. Taking the next step to ensure that your savings are invested properly and generating significant growth is critical. Quite simply, if you're not investing, you're likely losing money. The crucial next step is to ensure that your savings are invested properly and working hard to grow your money.

Retirement

One of the most illuminating books that Mr Sloth has read within the last few years is *The 100-Year Life*[19] by Andrew Scott and Lynda Gratton. The book explores the inevitable decisions that will have to be taken as a consequence of humans living increasingly longer lives.

It's critically important that we recognise and, indeed, are ready to take advantage of the simple reality that human beings are living longer. If you plan to retire at the traditional

19 Gratton, L., and Scott, A. *The 100-Year Life: Living and Working in an Age of Longevity* (Bloomsbury Business, 2017).

age of sixty-five, this means that you need to factor in a possible thirty-plus years of retirement (perhaps even longer, if you happen to be the beneficiary of advantageous genes or you are fortunate to reap the rewards of continuing advances in medicine).

This means there will be a tremendous amount of bills to pay for and if you intend to enjoy an active retirement, defined by travel and other leisure pursuits, you will need to plan accordingly. Therefore, it's vital to ensure that you have enough money to finance your retirement.

While it is certainly not the aim of Mr Sloth to invoke images of doom and gloom, it is nevertheless important to recognise that an inability to save and invest for your retirement could ultimately lead to you having to accept a lower standard of living and perhaps even having to work longer than you had originally intended.

Quite simply, the earlier you begin investing in the stock market, the greater opportunity that you will have to finance the retirement you deserve.

Compound Interest – the Snowball Effect

Okay, so we don't typically associate a sloth with snowballs, but stick with me on this one. Let's suppose you invested £1,000 into my 'Sloth Shakes' milkshake business. In the first year, the shares rose 10%. Your investment in my milkshakes business is now worth £1,100. You continue to hold shares in my business and in the second year, the shares appreciate another 10%. So, instead of your shares appreciating an additional £100 (just like in the first year), they appreciate an additional £10 because the £100 you gained in the first year grew by 10%, too. Therefore, after two years, your shares are worth £1,210.

So, what does any of this have to do with a snowball, I hear you ask? Well, I want you to imagine a snowball at the top of a hill covered in snow. As you roll this snowball down the hill, what's going to happen? Naturally, it picks up more snow. As it picks up more snow, it will become bigger and bigger, becoming much larger in size. This is where an analogy between a snowball and the realm of investment makes sense. Given time, even the smallest amount of money can grow to a massive amount. This process – of an item, whether it be snow or even money, getting bigger and bigger and bigger is known as compound interest.

The earlier you begin your investing journey, the better. Let's take a look now at an example that outlines two investors, Tom and Jerry. Tom begins investing at the age of fifteen, while Jerry doesn't begin investing until the age of thirty-five.

	Tom	Jerry
Begins investing at age:	15	35
Stops adding money at age:	30	65
Invests each year:	£1,000	£4,000
Invests a total of:	£15,000	£120,000
Total grows each year by:	10%	10%
Total worth at age 65:	£892,870	£657,976[20]

Jerry invests a total of £105,000 more than Jerry into the

---

20 The compound interest calculator on moneygeek.com was used for calculations.

stock market. To put it in another way, he invests *eight times* the original amount that Tom invested. However, he still finishes with almost £250,000 *less* than Tom. This is a quarter of a million pounds! How can this be?

The key, essential lesson to be learned from this example is the importance of time. Time is the crucial advantage that teenagers have over adults. Let compounding work in your favour! You'll learn a lot more about time later on in the book as it's one of my five bedrock principles.

The power of compounding is contingent upon three elements:

1. How long you let your money grow.
2. How much you invest (and how regularly).
3. What your growth rate is.

A Choice Enabler

Later on in this book, I will elaborate upon the importance of adhering to a 'buy-and-hold' approach to investing. In short, this means that you should be reluctant to sell your shares, as holding stocks for as long as possible will enable you to benefit greatly from the wonders of compound interest (remember the snowball that I referred to?). However, there may be an occasion when you wish to sell shares due to necessity or when an exciting opportunity has arisen that requires an injection of money.

For example, taking the latter point; at the age of fifty, you and your partner decide to take a break from work for a whole year. You were smart and started investing little by little in your late teens and after thirty-plus years of investing you can afford not to work for one year. During this period, you plan to spend precious time with your partner, read books and even travel a little bit more than usual. How could this be possible? Your opportunities in life will compound the earlier you start investing. Remember, wealth generation creates choice.

On this point, Ben Carlson, author of *A Wealth of Common Sense*, states:

> "Younger investors need to think in terms of what that future wealth can bring them – specifically, freedom and flexibility. The greatest thing that money can buy is time to do whatever it is that makes you happy. If you're forced to work later in life doing something you don't love to do for a pay check, that's not a fun scenario for a young person to consider… Whatever the most annoying part of your life is, use that as your motivation to save. If you hate your job, save enough money so you don't have to work for a boss that you don't like. If you want to travel the world, save enough to go wherever your heart desires. Think in terms of your future self."[21]

Historical Returns

Despite the hysteria sometimes associated with this method of wealth creation, the undeniable fact is that over a long time horizon, the stock market moves upwards.

According to Jeremy Siegel, a Wharton Business School professor, the average annualised return for the US stock

---

21 Carlson, B., *A Wealth of Common Sense: Why Simplicity Trumps Complexity in Any Investment Plan* (Bloomberg, 2015).

market between 1802 and 2012 was 8.1%. Moreover, applying the data from more recent history, we can learn from the same author that the average rate of return for the US stock market from 1946 to 2012 was 10.5%.[22]

Depending upon your source, whether it be online, in a book or word of mouth, the most often commonly quoted historical return for the stock market is in the range of 7–10%. If you want your money to overcome the harmful effects of inflation, then you should be aiming for an average annual return in this range. This book will outline a rational, common-sense (sloth-like) strategy that you can implement to fulfil this objective.

Democratisation of Information

There is now an abundance of information available to 21st-century investors. When they were young, my late mother and father and many other members of their generation were not fortunate enough to have access to the same degree of information that I now have access to. Therefore, you should be grateful and consider yourself lucky that the information age that you live in has radically improved the opportunities you now have to invest.

Again, as it's worth reiterating, these opportunities were not so accessible to previous generations. The internet has significantly contributed to the democratisation of information over the last twenty to thirty years and this certainly includes investing-related information.

---

22   Siegel, J., *Stocks for the Long Run: The Definitive Guide to Financial Market Returns & Long-Term Investment Strategies* (5th ed.), (Mc-Graw Hill: 2014).

Make a Deposit for the Future of Your Loved Ones

I love being a father to two children – a boy and a girl. One of the key reasons why I invest is to help to smooth their passage through life. It is my hope that the wealth I generate can help to reduce the financial burden of the respective paths that they choose to take within their lives, whether this is the availability of funds for things such as university tuition fees, a car or perhaps even a deposit for a house.

Here's an example. It's 2055 and university tuition fees have continued to rise in the decades after you purchased this book. You have one or more children at university age. The parents of your children's peers are fretting about the cost of sending their children to university. You are also naturally concerned about the cost of your child or children receiving a university education. However, the cost of a university education for your child will not impose a financial burden as great. This is because you have been wise and have grown a significant amount of money for this anticipated time in their life. How? Once again, by choosing to invest from a young age, you have generated enough wealth to ensure that your child will not leave university saddled with debt. Warren Buffett, arguably the world's most famous investor, neatly encapsulates the beauty underpinning this transference of wealth, this passing on of the financial baton, when he states: "Someone's sitting in the shade today because someone planted a tree a long time ago." So, remember this, if you have children or, if one day you intend to have children, investing enables you to make a deposit for their future.

Set a Positive Example

Your success as an investor can undoubtedly exert a positive compounding effect upon other people. This could be family members, friends, co-workers and even complete strangers. Talking to other people about the fruits of your investing success will likely cause a ripple effect. Taking myself as an example, I first became interested in investing after talking to my father-in-law, who was kind enough to share the wisdom that he had acquired within the field of investing.

In addition, listening to Andrew Hallam enabled me to learn more about the positive traits required to become a successful investor. As you become a more knowledgeable, seasoned investor, I encourage you to, in a sense, 'pay it forward' and pass on the actionable wisdom that you take from this book and other sources.

Taking Stock

So, at this juncture, it's probably time to take stock. What is the stock market? The stock market is a market for buying and selling shares in public companies. This process is made possible by a facility known as a stock exchange. The most noteworthy stock exchanges are the New York Stock Exchange, the London Stock Exchange (LSE) and the Japan Exchange Group (JPX).

Going Public

The listing of a company on a stock exchange means that the company has 'gone public' and shares can be sold to the general public. When a business is referred to as 'private', this means that the owners have not sold any stock to the general public. For example, Lego, a source of great entertainment for my children, is a private company.

Becoming a publicly traded company takes place through an IPO (Initial Public Offering). An IPO is the first time a company makes shares available to the public for purchase. The purchase of a company's shares enables the organisation to raise money to grow its business.

The IPO is a particularly exciting and eventful time for an organisation. It is a sign that the company has been deemed successful enough to become a prime candidate for further capital investment. For an organisation, there is also a significant amount of prestige associated with a listing on a stock exchange. Just as students graduate through sequentially aged educational tiers (nursery, primary, secondary, etc.), an IPO is a sign that an organisation has graduated to the next stage of its maturity.

Notable IPOs within the first quarter of the 21st century include Facebook (2012), Twitter (2013), Snapchat (2017), Uber (2019) and Airbnb (2020).

Types of Investors

The stock market is comprised of multiple participants. Let's now learn a little more about this diverse cast of characters.

Institutional Investors

Institutional investors play a significant role in the stock market. Institutional investors are organisations that buy and sell shares on behalf of their clients, such as pension funds, banks and insurance companies.

Institutional investors exert a tremendous influence on the stock market due to their ability to buy and sell vast amounts of shares. It is important to note that the money used by institutional investors has been generated through interactions with their clients. On the whole, institutional investors will invest on behalf of other people. For example, when individuals allocate a portion of their salary to a pension fund, they are entrusting that this money will be invested wisely by specific institutional investors. It is generally assumed that the supposed expertise of institutional investors will yield positive returns for the individual.

Individual Investors

Individual investors, sometimes known as retail investors, are investors such as you and I. Individual investors, unfairly, in my opinion, are often viewed as unsophisticated investors. Lacking the resources and the technology at the disposal of institutional investors, individual investors are subsequently considered to be at a distinct disadvantage. However, as I argue throughout this book, individual investors would be foolhardy to view themselves in such a poor light.

The FTSE, Dow Jones and the S&P 500

If you've seen a financial news report on television, you may have heard reference to the 'FTSE', the 'Dow Jones' or the 'S&P 500'. Let me now take the time to explain each of these terms.

The acronym 'FTSE' stands for the Financial Times Stock Exchange. The FTSE 100 refers to an index of 100 companies listed on the London Stock Exchange. The companies included are the 100 largest UK companies. Companies within this index include HSBC, JD Sports, Sainsbury's, Tesco and Vodafone group. Inclusion within this index is seen as a sign of prestige. If the businesses as a group rise in price, then the value of the FTSE 100 will rise.

Companies within the index that see a decline in their value can be demoted to the FTSE 250, an index that comprises the 101st to 350th largest companies listed on the London Stock Exchange. For example, in June 2019, EasyJet's market value became too small for it to be included in the FTSE 100 index and it therefore dropped out of the FTSE 100 and into the FTSE 250. Similarly, in September 2019, the same fate awaited Marks & Spencer as they dropped out of the FTSE 100. It was the first time the retailer had not been a FTSE 100 member since the index was created in 1984.

The Dow Jones refers to the 'Dow Jones Industrial Average', which is a stock market index that measures the performance of the stock market by using a group of thirty American companies, such as Disney, Apple, Coca-Cola, Visa and Microsoft, among many others. The index was founded in 1896. The index provided a way for Dow Jones to report on the health of the stock market. The companies within this index are considered to represent the crème de la crème of American business. When a company becomes less prominent, it will be dropped from the index. The Dow Jones is named after Charles Henry Dow and

Edward Jones. Dow, an American journalist, and Jones, an American statistician, co-founded Dow Jones & Company, an American financial information company. Interestingly, Charles Henry Dow also founded *The Wall Street Journal*, a leading financial publication.

The S&P 500 represents an index of 500 of the leading companies in the United States. Again, like the FTSE 100, if the businesses as a group rise in price, the S&P 500 index will rise, too. Due to its significantly larger size than the Dow, many deem it to be the best representation of the overall health of the US stock market. Sometimes referred to simply as the 'S&P', the index was founded in 1957. On a much larger scale, the Russell 3000 index is a benchmark of the entire US stock market. It provides a measurement of – you guessed it – the 3000 largest American companies.

Market Sectors

The companies listed on a stock exchange will be divided into sectors. Each sector constitutes a broad category of business. For instance, some of the sectors that you will find within the London Stock Exchange are banking, household utilities, retailers, healthcare and telecommunications – to name but a few. Each sector is defined by its own distinct characteristics. For example, within the healthcare sector, companies will spend heavily on research and development.

Bulls and Bears

Okay, so let's forget about our friend the sloth for a moment, as it's time to once again discuss the two animals most commonly associated with the stock market: the bull and the bear. Why are these two animals often referenced during discussions concerning the stock market?

Both terms are used to describe the sentiment concerning the stock market. A bull market is used to describe a stock market in which prices are rising and the overriding sentiment towards investing in the stock market is high. Conversely, a bear market is used to describe a stock market which is declining, with falling prices and weak overall sentiment.

The terms 'bullish' and 'bearish' are commonly used when describing investors' perceptions of investment opportunities. An investor who is keen to invest, expressing confidence and enthusiasm about the potential returns on offer, can be described as 'bullish'. In contrast, the phrase 'bearish' is used to describe an investor lacking in confidence.

Going Up, Going Down

A variety of factors can cause the share price of a company to either move up or down. Below, I have outlined some of the key reasons for both outcomes.

Reasons why a company's stock price may increase:

1. Sales and profits at the company increase.
2. In simple terms, more people want to own shares. As a result, more buyers than sellers drive the stock price to go up.
3. The company release an exciting new product.

4. The company wins a new contract. As a result, the anticipation of greater profits is now expected.

5. A Wall Street analyst upgrades the rating of the company, changing the recommendation from 'neutral' to 'buy' or 'buy' to 'strong buy'.

6. Global expansion plans are released, exciting existing and potential investors with the prospect of increased profits in the long term.

7. Quite simply, the rest of the stock market has risen.

8. Other stocks in the same industry increase.

Reasons why a company's stock price may decrease:

1. Sales and profits at the company are declining.

2. People don't want to own the stock. As a result, having fewer buyers than sellers causes the price to decrease.

3. An analyst on Wall Street downgrades the recommendation of the stock from 'buy' to 'hold' or from 'hold' to 'sell'.

4. The company loses a major customer.

5. An industry peer announces bad news.

6. A powerful company becomes a competitor.

7. A lawsuit is filed against the company.

8. Most of the stock market is down. This could be the result of a short-term recession or bear market.

The general stock market rises dramatically because of a relative minority of publicly traded companies. These companies are consistently successful and profitable, ensuring the continued growth of the stock market.

Therefore, in my opinion, while it is prudent to be optimistic about the long-term future of the stock market, one should be aware that purchasing individual stocks is risky. After all, how do you know that the specific individual company stocks that you have chosen will be successful? What advantage do you possess?

Types of Investments

- Stocks

When you purchase a stock, you're buying a stake in an actual, functioning business. A unit of a business's stock is called a share. When investors buy a stock on a stock exchange, they will be quoted the price of a single share. Then, they can choose to buy as many shares as they want, depending on the amount of money they have available.

Investors can make money by waiting for the share price to increase and then selling. Simply, the investor's profits are the difference between the purchase price and the sell price, minus any other expenses. These profits are often referred to as capital gains.

- Generating Money

When a company generates money, it can choose to retain this capital as earnings or share that profit with its shareholders. When a company chooses to share part of this profit with its shareholders, it does this in the form of a dividend payment. The company's board of directors will determine the precise percentage of its earnings that should be allocated to shareholders. Dividends are typically paid on a quarterly basis, although some companies may make semi-annual or even annual payments.

Companies offer dividend payments for numerous reasons. Naturally, it is appealing to investors to receive additional income, so the distribution of dividends can make a company's stock appear more attractive. Furthermore, many investors could deem a company's dividend payments to be a sign of positive financial health, which in turn leads to further investment, a higher stock price and increased dividend payments in the future.

Companies that pay a dividend are invariably older, more mature businesses. However, broadly speaking, newer, rapidly growing companies often choose not to pay dividends. Quite simply, the reason for this is because these businesses believe that the best use of their capital is to reinvest in their business to ignite more growth.

- Bonds

A bond is a form of investment that represents a loan from an investor to a borrower. This loan is usually to a government or a company. Although they usually return less than stocks, bonds are usually less volatile and can therefore perform a stabilising role on your portfolio.

In the chapter entitled 'Considerations for Your Sloth Portfolio', I elaborate on the important role that bonds can play in your portfolio.

- Exchange-Traded Funds (ETFs)

An exchange-traded fund represents a collection of stocks or bonds that can be bought or sold on a stock exchange.

Most ETFs track a reputable index such as the S&P 500 or the FTSE 100.

Throughout this book, I wholeheartedly endorse index-tracking ETFs. Here are the key reasons why:

- Low cost (management charges typically range from 0.10% to 0.50%).
- Easy to buy on major stock exchanges such as the London Stock Exchange and the New York Stock Exchange.
- Convenient and accessible for individual investors (low starting capital).
- Widely diversified, thereby meaning that this is a less risky way to participate in the continued, anticipated growth of the stock market (in the long term).
- Investing in a broad-based ETF, such as a globally diversified ETF (containing companies from around the world), is inherently less volatile than purely investing in your own, smaller portfolio of individual stocks.

The final point above is particularly key. This is because one of the chief reasons why investing in a smaller portfolio of individual stocks is risky is because of the volatility associated with this form of investment. For example, it is not uncommon for individual companies to see their share price plummet, perhaps by as much as 30% in a single day (and sometimes more) in the event of declining sales or perhaps a revised, unfavourable update from a stock analyst. However, by investing in a globally diversified ETF, you are reducing what I term the 'volatility potential' of your portfolio. This therefore increases the likelihood that you will not be deterred from investing (as you have chosen to invest in a manner that is inherently less volatile) and will continue to have 'skin in the game' – i.e. by continuing to invest year after year, decade after decade.

• Hitch a Ride on the Haystack!

Jack Bogle, one of the members of FIFI (my Five International Fantasy Investors, referred to earlier in the book), once uttered some of my favourite words about the ease in which you can capture the aggregate growth of the stock market as a whole (rather than looking to profit from specific individual stocks). Here they are: "Don't look for the needle in the haystack. Just buy the haystack!"[23]

• Gold

Committing money to gold has historically been a highly speculative investment. Its volatility and associated price fluctuations make it a particularly unpredictable form of investment. Indeed, some would argue that it is not a form of investment at all. Warren Buffett has been particularly scathing of gold, stating that it is not a 'productive asset' (unlike stocks).

• Commodities

Basic raw materials such as crude oil, natural gas, metals and other natural resources are commonly referred to in the investment world as 'commodities'. The price of

---

23 Bogle, J C, *The Little Book of Common Sense Investing: The Only Way to Guarantee Your Fair Share of Stock Market Returns* (Wiley, 2007).

commodities can fluctuate wildly and can be extremely difficult to understand. An inherent difficulty with investment in commodities is their sensitivity to geopolitical decision-making. Finally, there are varied factors that can affect the long-term supply of a specific commodity, such as natural disasters, which adds yet another layer of complexity to this form of investment.

• Property

Investing in property has traditionally been a common form of investment for many citizens in my home country, the United Kingdom. There are potentially two ways to elicit a return on a property investment:

1. Renting – You can receive an income by letting out your property.
2. Selling for a profit – You buy a property and then sell it later after the purchase price has appreciated.

Though commonly a favourable form of investment for many investors around the world, investing in property comes with some risks. For example, investing in property is not a liquid form of investment, which means that it can take a considerable amount of time to sell your property, making it difficult to immediately access the capital that you invested in the property. In addition, property investment can be demanding on your time. For instance, the initial search for a property can often take a significant amount of time, with many factors that need to come under consideration. Moreover, maintenance work on the property can exact a further toll on both your time and your potential profits (particularly if you are looking to let your property). Finally, if you require a mortgage to purchase your property, there are further risks such as whether you will receive enough rent to cover the mortgage payments and, in a worst-case scenario, a bank can take back the property from you if you do not keep pace with the mortgage repayments.

Having taken all this into consideration, the sloth investor does not entirely dismiss property as a form of investment. Instead, the sloth investor considers property to be just one of a diverse range of investments.

Mr Sloth's Summary:

- There are numerous reasons why it is important to invest. Chief among them is the opportunity it gives you to exert greater directionality upon your life – i.e. the opportunity to retire earlier.
- Appreciate the snowball – the impact of compound interest snowballs over time. It's important to remember, though, that compound interest can transform lives, for good and for bad (think here about the compounding effect of credit card fees). Enabling compound interest to work in your favour – i.e. through broadly investing in the stock market – can have a truly transformative impact on your life.
- A bull market is used to describe a stock market in which prices are rising and the overriding sentiment towards investing in the stock market is high. Conversely, a bear market is used to describe a stock market that is declining, with falling prices and weak overall sentiment.
- There are multiple reasons why an individual stock – i.e. a company's share price – can increase or decrease, making it a particularly rocky ride for such investors. Investing in a more broad-based manner (you'll learn more about this in the section called 'Own the World' in Chapter 5) enables you, the retail investor, to capture the growth of the stock market in aggregate, rather than relying on individual stocks.

The Five Bedrock Principles of the Sloth Investor

Simplicity

"The more complex the world around us becomes, the more simplicity we must seek in order to realise our financial goals. Please underrate neither the majesty of simplicity nor its proven effectiveness as a long-term strategy for productive investing. Simplicity is the master key to financial success."[24]

John C Bogle

At first glance, the field of investing can appear daunting. It's not uncommon to hear some people utter phrases such as:

- "It's a numbers game and I'm not great at maths..."
- "It would put me out of my depth..."

24   Bogle, John C, *Investing with Simplicity*, a speech for The Personal Finance Conference, *The Washington Post*, Washington, D.C., on January 30th, 1999.

- "No one in my family has ever invested before…"
- "It's like gambling…"

Such phrases reveal an imposter syndrome that is a common feature within the mindset of many people. What's the cause of this? As you would expect, various reasons can be given. Could it be the all too often hyperbolic, hysterical depiction of the stock market in the mainstream media? Is it the jargon that some people associate with the stock market? Or perhaps it's simply the inexperience factor.

Can you blame some people for lacking the confidence to invest? This is particularly true when someone has never been given the opportunity to learn about how to grow their money over a sustained period of time. In this regard, the education system is guilty of not preparing people for the realities of life, particularly the necessity to grow one's money over a lifetime.

Demystifying Investing

Whatever the reason for someone's reluctance to invest, one of the chief aims of the five bedrock principles that follow in this section is to demystify investing.

To demystify means to make clearer or to simplify. Within the field of investing, it's important to note that there are no prizes awarded for difficulty. Instead, as I outline in the 'Headstrong' section of the bedrock principles, simply avoiding the unwise, foolhardy errors made by other investors will enable you to attain success as an investor.

Contrary to what some may think, investing doesn't require an IQ above 130, a university degree or an ability to number crunch an incessant amount of numerical figures. Instead, an understanding of five bedrock principles – Simplicity, Low Fees, Owning the World, Time in the Market and Headstrong – can enable you to develop the belief that you can become a confident, rationally informed investor or, what I prefer to call, a 'sloth investor'.

Don't Trade. Keep It Simple: Invest!

To those that are new to the stock market, and particularly those unfamiliar with the bedrock principles that I endorse, the inclination to trade stocks can be tempting. One must be aware of the perils of trading, though. In a July 2020 interview with MarketWatch, Burton Malkiel, author of *A Random Walk Down Wall Street*, states:

> "To go and day trade and think that you are investing, that's what I think is absolutely wrong and is likely to be simply disastrous for people. All the evidence is that day traders, in general, lose money."[25]

Malkiel's statement is supported by the findings of a study that looked into the trading activity of almost 70,000 households. The study found that the 20% of investors that

---

25 'Investing legend Burton Malkiel on day-trading millennials, the end of the 60/40 portfolio and more' by Andrea Riquier on *MarketWatch*. Published on 15th July 2020 – [marketwatch.com/story/investing-legend-burton-malkiel-on-day-trading-millennials-the-end-of-the-6040-portfolio-and-more-2020-06-22].

traded most frequently earned an average return of more than 7% lower than the average household in the study.[26]

Interestingly, the tendency towards trading can particularly afflict those in upper management positions. It would seem that the feeling of responsibility and power accompanied by holding such a position comes also with a sense of overconfidence. For example, one study explored the investment performance of such individuals and found that they developed overconfidence due to their high-powered status, which subsequently led to increased trading in their portfolios, resulting in less-than-average performance in the returns of their investment account.[27]

Trading is commonly characterised by a frantic, high-octane, rapid process of buy and sells. A quote from the 1995 film, *Heat* – one of my favourite movies – succinctly summarises the thrill of trading: "For me, the action is the juice."[28]

These words are uttered by Michael (played by Tom Sizemore) to Neil (played by Robert De Niro). Though not directly about investing, the above quote serves as a useful metaphor as it neatly encapsulates the intense thrill that individuals generate during the process of trading. This is because, for traders, there can be no doubt that action is their juice – the perfect tonic to quench their insatiable

26 Barber, B., Odean, T., Lee, Y. and Liu, Y, 'Just How Much Do Individual Investors Lose By Trading?', *Haas School of Business*, October 2006.

27 Mitchell, O. and Utkus, S., 'Lessons from Behavioral Finance for Retirement Plan Design', Wharton Pension Research Council Working Paper (2003).

28 Mann, M., *Heat* (Warner Bros, 1995).

thirst for activity. By now, I hope you've realised that this constantly simmering concoction, this dizzying beverage that traders choose to consume and devour on a daily basis, is a potent, heady and altogether potentially dangerous mix of rapidly bought, quick-fire buy and sells.

Refreshing as this may be to traders, is it really a healthy juice for you – a sloth investor – to consume? Should this adrenaline-inducing beverage be the tonic that quenches your thirst for capital appreciation? No, instead, I strongly urge you to wholeheartedly and enthusiastically guzzle on an altogether calmer, common-sense cocktail of sloth investor bedrock principles otherwise known as:

- Simplicity
- Low fees.
- A commitment to a globally diversified portfolio.
- An unrelenting desire for the importance of time *in* the market.
- A headstrong temperament.

The Big Sloth?

As you may have gathered by my previous reference to *Heat*, I'm a major movie fan and I particularly enjoy watching movies that explore the world of finance. As such, I'm a fan of movies such as *The Big Short* and *Flash Boys*, both of which are big-screen adaptations of books written by Michael Lewis – an acclaimed author who also had an earlier career working within the financial industry.

Naturally, given both the expanse of his writing on

the topic and his aforementioned time spent working in the industry, you may have expected Michael Lewis to be someone who utilises sophisticated techniques to invest. However, perhaps somewhat surprisingly, this is not the case. Several years ago, in an interview with MarketWatch in 2016, he stated:

> "I've always been a boring and conservative investor. I own index funds, and I don't time the market… I put it away and I don't look at it very much… I think the best way is a low-cost index fund. I do not think people really should be making individual stock picks with their savings. I think that's generally been demonstrated to be not such a good idea. If you want to do it as entertainment like gambling – like you bet on football games – fine, but I think you're better off in a low-cost index fund, like a Vanguard index fund."[29]

Simplicity > Complexity

After reading about each of the bedrock principles in this section of the book, I hope you are able to develop an appreciation of the simplicity of the approach to investing that both Michael Lewis and the sloth investor takes. It seems that many people feel uneasy when something seems simple. This is because it feels that everything that gives a reward has to be difficult and requires an intense amount of action.

29 'The Big Short author Michael Lewis says this is where you should put your money' by Maria LaMagna. Published on *MarketWatch* on 14th December 2016 – [marketwatch.com/story/the-big-short-author-michael-lewis-says-this-is-where-you-should-put-your-money-2016-12-07].

John Reed writes in his book, *Succeeding*:

> "When you first start to study a field, it seems like you have to memorise a zillion things. You don't. What you need is to identify the core principles that govern the field. The million things you thought you had to memorise are simply various combinations of the core principles."[30]

Investing is the same. At first, it may appear that the field of investing is governed by complexity. Fortunately, this is not the case. Adhering to the simple bedrock principles that underpin the sloth investor's approach to investing will equip you with the investing tools that you should have learned at school. Constructing an investment portfolio that is governed by simplicity has several distinct benefits:

- It will enable you to reduce the fees that you pay.
- It's easy to maintain, enabling you to adopt a SWAN (Sleep Well At Night) approach to investing.
- It reduces your chances of making an error.

Finally, and perhaps most significantly, creating a simple, sloth-like portfolio will allow you to spend time on the aspects of your life that really matter. Here's a simple acronym to close this section on simplicity, the first bedrock principle of the sloth investor.

Kiss – **K**eep **I**t **S**imple **S**loth!

---

30   Reed, J T, *Succeeding* (2003).

Mr Sloth's Summary:

Well, this section of the book addresses simplicity, so let's keep Mr Sloth's summary nice and simple. Here are some key takeaways for you, dear reader, on simplicity, the first bedrock principle of the sloth investor.

- Simplicity > Complexity
- Inactivity > Activity
- Investing > Trading

Low Fees

"Huge institutional investors, viewed as a group, have
long underperformed the unsophisticated index-fund
investor who simply sits tight for decades. A major
reason has been fees."[31]

Warren Buffett

From Sloth to Sleuth

When tasked with considering the investment vehicles they
should invest their hard-earned money in, sloth investors
turn sleuth. Turning sleuth-like, a sloth investor considers the
merits of both high-fee, actively managed funds and their low-
fee counterpart, the ETF tracker (that tracks an index fund).

The first bedrock principle of a sloth investor is simplicity.
Therefore, it should naturally follow that a belief in simplicity
– a 'less is more', inactive approach to investing – shouldn't
require high fees. This line of thinking is correct.

Unfortunately, though, many investors commit the
time-worn error of paying high fees by investing in actively

31   Buffett, Warren, *Berkshire Hathaway Golden Anniversary Letter to
     Shareholders 2015* (27th February 2015) – [berkshirehathaway.com/
     letters/2014ltr.pdf].

managed funds. Actively managed funds are either run by an individual portfolio manager, co-managers or a team of managers. You, the investor, will pay a high fee for an actively managed fund because these 'professionals' engage in research, market forecasting and other labour-intensive practices. Remember, the sloth investor believes in a minimal approach to investing – i.e. that is *not* labour intensive.

Typically, this is how an actively managed fund works:

- You send money to the fund company.
- This fund company combines your money with other investors' money into their active fund.
- The manager/s of this fund regularly buy and sell stocks within this fund with the desired aim that this will result in profits for investors.

A key reason for the relatively high cost of actively managed funds is because of this regular process of buying and selling. For instance: on Monday, a fund manager may purchase Facebook shares and sell GlaxoSmithKline shares, but then buy back the GlaxoSmithKline shares two months later. As humans, our bias tends to lean towards action. However, within the field of investing, inaction beats action.

A sloth investor's scepticism towards actively managed funds is dictated by rational, statistically informed data. To be clear, can actively managed funds beat the return of index funds over a one- to five-year time horizon? Yes, of course; this is a fact that I would not deny. However, over an investment lifetime, consisting of multiple decades, the odds of an actively managed fund consistently outperforming an index fund are slim.

Indeed, the performance of the vast majority of actively managed funds pales into insignificance when compared to the long-term return of index funds. Richard Ferri, author of *The Power of Passive Investing – More Wealth With Less Work*, states:

> "Winning actively managed funds are only a small percentage of the total funds outstanding, and identifying these winning active funds in advance is nearly impossible. There are no proven methodologies that accurately predict future winning active funds. Of course, that doesn't stop many market gurus who will claim to have a winning active fund picking formula that they'll sell you for a fee."[32]

Similarly, writing in his 2021 book *Trillions*, author Robin Wigglesworth has this to state on what the data tells us for someone's chances of consistently performing well with active funds:

> "Data is a hard taskmaster, but has consistently shown that while someone might get lucky for a few years, very few do so in the long run."[33]

Despite the small odds, a significant number of investors continue to hold the mistaken belief that paying high fees

---

32 Ferri, R., *The Power of Passive Investing: More Wealth with Less Work* (Gildan Media: 2020).

33 Wigglesworth, Robin, *Trillions: How a Band of Wall Street Renegades Invented the Index Fund and Changed Finance Forever* (Penguin, 2021).

to invest in actively managed funds will result in superior performance, as they naively believe that the 'professionals' who manage these funds will guide them towards the best investments. Quite simply, though, there is countless evidence to demonstrate that this is not the case. In an article titled 'The Rise and Fall of Performance Investing' in the *Financial Analysts Journal*, Charles D. Ellis states:

> "The long-term data repeatedly documents that investors would benefit by switching from active performance investing to low-cost indexing."[34]

In his landmark investment book, *A Random Walk Down Wall Street*, Burton Malkiel writes:

> "A blindfolded monkey throwing darts at a newspaper's financial pages could select a portfolio that would do just as well as one carefully selected by experts."[35]

The Price You Pay for the 'Professional Touch' – Shining a Spotlight on Fees

According to Morningstar, the majority of actively managed funds have an OCF (ongoing charges figure) of between 0.5% and 1.5%. They also state that 7.6% of funds possess an OCF of 2% or higher. In comparison, passively managed

---

34 'The Rise and Fall of Performance Investing' by Charles D Ellis. Published in *Financial Analysts Journal* on 28th March 2018 – 10.2469/faj.v70.n4.4.

35 Malkiel, Burton, *A Random Walk Down Wall Street: The Time Tested Strategy for Successful Investing* (12th edition); (Recorded Books, 2019).

funds (the approach to investing advocated by Mr Sloth) are much cheaper. Morningstar states that almost 90% have an OCF of less than 0.5%.[36]

Let's now shine a light upon the exact reasons for the fees associated with an actively managed fund:

- Investment-management fees – These fees are related to the cost of active managers researching and selecting investments for the actively managed fund that you have chosen to invest in.
- Administration fees – These fees are associated with the cost of maintaining a record of your investment.
- Performance fees – Some actively managed funds charge a performance fee. This fee will be a pre-assigned % in excess of a target level.
- Fund trading fees – These fees are related to the cost of buying and selling the shares that comprise the actively managed fund. Due to the frequent buying and selling associated with actively managed funds, this fee is significantly greater than index trackers that alter their investments far less frequently.

'Superstar or Subpar?'

In my native country of the United Kingdom, it has not been uncommon for fund managers to be portrayed in hyperbolic form, characterised as superstars that will perform heroic

---

36 'A Closer Look at UK Fund Costs' by Grace Oliver. Published on the *Morningstar* – https://www.morningstar.co.uk/uk/ news/215822/a-closer-look-at-uk-fund-costs.aspx

feats with customers' money. Indeed, huge swathes of the British financial media should accept responsibility for the role that they have played in compelling retail investors to invest in high-fee, actively managed funds headed by such supposed 'superstar' fund managers.

In the UK, one such 'star' was Neil Woodford. Woodford, once a famed stock-picker and spearhead of Woodford Investment Management, suffered a spectacular fall from grace in 2019 when his flagship actively managed fund, 'Woodford Equity Income Fund', was placed into liquidation. The result was that many people lost large amounts of money from their retirement pot. Hargreaves Lansdown, a leading British financial services company, with an imposing online presence and influence, consistently recommended the fund to consumers.

Buffett's Bet

Warren Buffett firmly believes that the simplicity of low-fee index funds is the approach to investing that consumers should adhere to. In 2008, Buffett set a challenge to the hedge fund industry, which consisted of numerous active funds. Buffett, believing that the fees charged by these funds are exorbitant, bet that a simple S&P 500 index fund would beat a hand-picked portfolio of hedge funds over a duration of ten years. The winner? You guessed right: Buffett's choice of the simple S&P 500 index fund (the Vanguard S&P 500 Admiral fund). In his 2016 Berkshire Hathaway shareholder letter, Buffett has this to say about the active managers of these funds:

"I'm certain that in almost all cases the managers at both levels were honest and intelligent people. But the results for their investors were dismal – really dismal. And, alas, the huge fixed fees charged by all of the funds and funds-of-funds involved – fees that were totally unwarranted by performance – were such that their managers were showered with compensation over the nine years that have passed… The bottom line: When trillions of dollars are managed by Wall Streeters charging high fees, it will usually be the managers who reap outsized profits, not the clients. Both large and small investors should stick with low-cost index funds."[37]

Buffett's point about the profits accrued by these active fund managers chimes with the sentiment of a classic investing book entitled, *Where Are the Customers' Yachts?* by Fred Schwed. This book rails against the disgracefully high fees that are charged by the active fund industry.

A Conspiracy Against the Laity

In *The Doctor's Dilemma*[38], a play by George Bernard Shaw (Irish playwright and Nobel Prize winner), we hear the phrase 'a conspiracy against the laity'. What does this phrase mean and what relevance does it have to investing?

Well, essentially, the phrase refers to the methods used by professionals, whether they be investing, managerial or otherwise, to obtain advantage in their interactions with

---

37   Buffett, Warren, *Berkshire Hathaway Annual Letter to Shareholders 2016* (2016) – [berkshirehathaway.com/letters/2016ltr.pdf].

38   Shaw, G B., *The Doctor's Dilemma* (1st ed.). (CreateSpace Independent Publishing Platform: 2014).

others by using their position (and power) to gain control. Those in a 'professional' position perhaps acquire this position by using language as a tool to further cement their status as the all-knowing entity within a particular field. For example, 'financial professionals' might achieve this status through their use of opaque, complex phrases that only serve to mystify and confuse the novice investor.

Simply put, faced with a barrage of investment jargon, many novice investors develop an 'imposter syndrome', leading them to place the domain of investing in a box marked 'too difficult'. As a consequence, this then provides the novice investor – perhaps with little prior knowledge of investing – with some degree of justification in paying high fees as they're led to believe that the realm of investing is too complex and crammed full of jargon.

Furthermore, the confidence exuded by many investment professionals can often compel novice investors to arrive at the false assumption that their hard-earned income is better off in the hands of 'the pros'. However, it is important to be streetwise and wary when dealing with a confident-sounding financial advisor. In his book, *The Little Book of Behavioral Investing*, author James Montier writes:

> "Our species has an unfortunate habit of using confidence as a proxy for skill… we want people to sound confident. In fact, we love people to sound confident. Psychologists have repeatedly found that people prefer those who sound confident and are even willing to pay more for confident (but inaccurate) advisors."[39]

39   Montier, J., *The Little Book of Behavioral Investing: How not to be your own worst enemy*, (1st ed.), (Wiley, 2010).

Do Financial 'Professionals' Know Best?

As consumers, we are conditioned to believe that the more we pay, the higher the quality of results. Moreover, in most walks of life, we place our confidence in the professionals.

Naturally, if you require a tooth to be extracted, you visit a dentist. If you experience back pain, then you'll visit a doctor. Invariably, you'll walk away from the dental practice or doctor's surgery feeling content. However, it's important to understand the distinct difference between the field of investing and other professional domains. This is because the investing world is a prime example of when the 'professionals' may not achieve the best results. So, it's critical that you take this important distinction into account before you become duped into paying high fees to professional advisers. On this point of professional expertise (or lack of), it's perhaps best to leave the final words to Warren Buffett. At Berkshire Hathaway's annual meeting in 2006, this is what he stated:

> "If your wife is going to have a baby, you're going to be better off if you call an obstetrician than if you do it yourself. And if your plumbing pipes are clogged, you're probably better off calling a plumber. Most professions have value added to them above what the laymen can accomplish themselves. In aggregate, the investment profession does not do that… so you have a huge group of people making – I put the estimate as $140 billion a year – that, in aggregate, are and can only accomplish what somebody can do in ten minutes a year by themselves."

Mr Sloth's Summary:

- In most aspects of life, you pay a higher fee for superior service. As consumers, we are conditioned to believe that the more we pay, the higher the quality of results. However, this is yet again one key way that the realm of investing is different. It's important to remember that the compounding effect of high fees can have a disastrous impact on your portfolio.
- Remain wary of the high fees charged by so-called 'superstar' funds. A small number of actively managed funds can perform well over a short duration. However, over an investment lifetime, consisting of multiple decades, the odds of an actively managed fund consistently outperforming an index fund are slim.

Own the World

> "By expanding the portfolio beyond the home market, we achieve much greater diversification in our investments. This is because we spread our investments over a larger number of stocks but, more importantly, because those stocks are based in different geographical areas and local economies."[40]

Lars Kroijer

Okay, so by now you're probably thinking, 'I need to keep things simple, pay low fees, but... what do I actually need to buy?' The following bedrock principle will help you understand the rationale that underpins what the sloth investor should buy.

The Letter 'S' – to the Power of Three!

To keep things simple, let's consider three options for how an investor could choose to invest their money in the stock market. They each begin with the letter 'S'.

---

40 Kroijer, Lars, *Investing Demystified: How to Invest Without Speculation and Sleepless Nights*, (2nd ed), (FT Publishing International, 2017).

Stocks

Sectors

States (countries)

Let's now take each in turn.

• Stocks

Browse through the business section of broadsheet newspapers and you're bound to find recommendations for the latest top stock. Following such a strategy can potentially be a perilous course of action, though. When investing your hard-earned money, it's important to consider the concept of advantage. For example, what advantage do you possess in understanding which stock tips to dismiss and which stock tips to proceed and purchase? In his stellar investment book, *The Simple Path to Wealth*, JL Collins states:

> "The harsh truth is, I can't pick winning individual
> stocks and you can't either. Nor can the vast majority
> who claim they can. It is extraordinarily difficult,
> expensive and a fool's errand. Having the humility
> to accept this will do wonders for your ability to
> accumulate wealth."[41]

Echoing this belief, in a July 2020 interview with MarketWatch, Burton Malkiel, author of the investment classic, *A Random Walk Down Wall Street*, states:

---

41 Collins, J L, *The Simple Path to Wealth: Your road map to financial independence and a rich, free life* (1st Edition); (CreateSpace Independent Publishing Platform, 2016).

> "For me, investing means buy and hold… the thesis
> of *Random Walk* was that you are much better off not
> buying individual stocks, but buying an index fund."[42]

Even if you do experience some initial success with the selection of individual stocks, how can you be sure that the specific individual stocks that you purchase will perform well year after year after year? Are you privy to information about how the company will add to its competitive advantage? It's important to stress that no matter how much effort you commit towards learning everything there is to know about a business, its growth prospects and the markets in which it competes, there will always be a significant amount of information that you don't know. Recognising and being humble about what you don't know is a key attribute of the sloth investor. Fundamentally, the likelihood of you picking a winning stock is small while your odds of selecting a loser is significantly large.[43]

In recent years, there has been an increase in the number of YouTube channels devoted to offering stock tips.[44] Despite the polished production values of the videos created by these YouTube content creators, it is important to recognise the

42 'Investing legend Burton Malkiel on day-trading millennials, the end of the 60/40 portfolio and more' by Andrea Riquier on *MarketWatch*. Published on 15th July 2020 – [marketwatch.com/story/investing-legend-burton-malkiel-on-day-trading-millennials-the-end-of-the-6040-portfolio-and-more-2020-06-22].

43 'The Agony & The Ecstasy: The Risks and Rewards of a Concentrated Stock Position' by Michael Cembalest. Published in *Eye on the Market*, March 2021.

44 'The New Way to Invest — Just Click on to YouTube' by Yasmin Choudhury. Published in *The Times* on April 10th 2022 – [the-times.co.uk/article/the-new-way-to-invest-just-click-on-to-youtube-8frh7rfrd].

difficulty of selecting the specific stocks that will perform well on a year-to-year basis. How can you be sure that the individuals responsible for creating this content are worthy of consideration? What advantage do they have? Does the ability of this YouTube creator to create a well-crafted and slick video necessarily make them a master stock-picker?

The final point I would like to add about individual stocks is the high degree of volatility associated with them. "Wait a second," I hear you ask, "isn't a degree of volatility an inherent feature of investing in the stock market in general?" Yes, that's true.

However, investing in individual stocks can *really* be volatile. For instance, purely based upon the news of a negative earnings report or a disparaging news article, it's not unusual for an individual stock to see a double-digit percentage drop in its value. For example, in April 2022, the share price of Netflix slumped by around 35%.[45] This primarily occurred because the company reported a sharp drop in subscribers.

Now, of course, the opposite can certainly be true, whereby individual stocks can also be subject to significant, sudden price increases. The question is, in addition to being able to consistently find 'winning' individual stocks, do you have the stomach to handle the potential plummeting percentage falls that can afflict them?

---

45 '$50bn wiped off Netflix's value as subscribers quit' by Daniel Thomas. Published on *BBC News* on 21st April 2022 – [bbc.com/news/business-61173561].

- Sectors

Shortly before writing this specific section of the book, I had been reading an online investing forum. On the forum, someone posted a question that went something like this: "I've heard that now is a great time to invest in the uranium industry, what do you think?"

In thinking about this question, I immediately reached for my crystal ball, but then realised that I (unfortunately) don't possess one. When looking to invest money, it can be tempting to look for a particular niche section of the stock market that could potentially benefit, whether this be due to rising demand, new trends, etc.

Investors that choose to allocate their money in this way are essentially investing in a *sector*. A sector is a segment of the market that represents a specific part of the economy.

Broadly speaking, here are the eleven sectors of the stock market:

- Energy
- Materials
- Industrials
- Consumer Discretionary
- Consumer Staples
- Healthcare
- Financials
- Information Technology
- Telecommunication Services
- Utilities
- Property

What would my response have been to the individual that posted a question about investing heavily in the energy sector – i.e. in uranium? Quite simply, my response would have been that it is foolhardy to concentrate one's capital in a particular sector of the market. In case you are wondering, although I did not respond to the original poster, numerous other investors did respond and they outlined a similar sentiment to my own.

It can be tempting to allocate one's money to the next hot sector, the slice of the economy that looks set to benefit from a new technology or new political trends. Following the financial crisis of 2008, technology stocks and particularly the so-called FAANG stocks (Facebook, Amazon, Apple, Netflix, Google) performed well.

Consequently, some investors may be tempted to predict that investing in the tech sector could continue to be a 'sure-fire' investing strategy. However, as with investing in individual stocks, how can we possibly know which sectors will perform well in the coming decades? Again, what advantage do you possess? The simple answer is that, without a crystal ball, it is incredibly difficult to make such predictions. Instead, the sloth investor invests in a diversified stock portfolio, across most, if not all, of the aforementioned sectors.

• States

As I write this book, we are roughly one quarter of the way through the 21st century. Contemporary political commentators often like to make grand pronouncements about which country (state) will come to dominate the current century. For instance, will America continue to exert its considerable political and economic dominance on the world stage throughout the 21st century? Or will this, perhaps, be the Chinese century, as many predict?

A Lesson from the Far East

It can be tempting for investors to analyse the political and economic factors that affect specific countries and to then allocate their money accordingly. For example, wanting to ride the crest of a wave, a significant number of investors can make the mistake of heavily concentrating their portfolio in a specific country, purely because that country has been performing well for an extended period of time. In this regard, Japan provides us with a textbook example of overexposure to a specific country's stock market.

Despite its obliteration at the end of the Second World War, the Japanese economy performed strongly in the post-war period. Indeed, during this time, Japan became the world's second-largest economy (after the United States). It would have been easy for investors, particularly Japanese investors, to get carried away by this 'economic miracle' and to invest a significantly high percentage of their portfolio in the Japanese market. However, over the past thirty years, the size of the domestic stock market in Japan has shrunk considerably, leading to disappointing returns. Therefore, quite simply, it would have been far more preferable for Japanese investors to diversify their portfolio geographically, instead of adhering to a home bias by over allocating their portfolio to their domestic stock market.

Japanese investors that continued to invest heavily in their nation's stock market post-1990 would have suffered from the effects of what is known as 'home bias'.

Home Bias

It's important to note that 'home bias' is the Achilles heel of many of my compatriots in the United Kingdom.

Despite the fact that the British stock market represents around 4 to 5% of the global stock market, many Brits continue to overweight their investments into their home stock market. For example, it's not unusual for many Brits to devote the entirety of their portfolio to their domestic stock market. What's the reason for this? Perhaps it's because of familiarity, with these investors believing that they inherently understand the companies in their home market.

British investors that are guilty of over investing in their home market need to question the rationale that underpins this approach. For example, what evidence is there to suggest that the British stock market will consistently outperform other stock markets?

Home Bias Affects Investors Around the Globe

The phenomenon of home bias isn't just restricted to British investors. In a 2017 paper by Vanguard entitled, 'The global case for strategic asset allocation and an examination of home bias',[46] the company reported on the fact that,

---

46 'The global case for strategic asset allocation and an examination of home bias' by Brian J. Scott, CFA; James Balsamo; Kelly N. McShane; Christos Tasopoulos. Vanguard Research, *Financial Advisor*, February 2017 – [fa-mag.com/userfiles/white_papers/wp_5.pdf].

on average, Canadian investors allocated 59% of their portfolios to their home market. This is despite the fact that the Canadian equity market accounted for only 3.4% of the global equity market (as of 31st December 2014). The data is even more striking for Australian investors. Despite the fact that the Australian stock market accounted for only 2.4% of the global stock market (again, as of 31st December 2014), Australian investors, on average, allocated 66.5% of their portfolios to their domestic stock market.

The Dangers of Home Bias

Although some investors may, on the one hand, feel more comfortable allocating a significantly high proportion of their portfolio to their domestic equity market, it is important to note the pitfalls of this approach. An overexposure to one's domestic stock market is problematic because this could result in an investor having little or no stake in prominent global businesses that are located outside of their home market.

In addition, a portfolio containing a heavy concentration of domestic companies is likely to suffer from a reduced exposure to a wide range of sectors. For instance, according to data by Siblis research, the FTSE 100, a leading index of British companies, has an exposure of just 1.41% to information technology stocks (as of 31st December 2021). In contrast, a globally diversified index tracker typically has an allocation of around 20% to this sector.

Question: How Should I Invest?
Answer: Invest in a low-fee, globally diversified index tracker.

Within the previous section, my contention was that individual stock-picking, favouring certain sectors of the market, or perhaps even an overexposure to one's domestic stock market are strategies that contain inherent flaws.

A Globally Diversified Portfolio – a Sloth Investor's Approach to Investing

So, what is the sloth investor's approach to investing?

The sloth investor invests proportionally, based on the market capitalisation of the global stock market. In other words, the sloth investor owns a global index fund tracker that is allocated according to the percentage representations of the countries that constitute the global stock market.

So, let's take the British stock market. If the British stock market roughly represents 4 to 5% of the overall value of the global stock market, then the sloth investor recognises that around 4 to 5% of their equity (stock) investment needs to be in the British stock market.

Likewise, the United States represents around 55% of the global stock market. Consequently, you guessed it, the sloth investor strives to ensure that around 55% of their equity portfolio is in the stock market of the United States.

Understanding Your 'Circle of Competence'

The sloth investor is a humble investor, deferential to their 'circle of competence' and therefore willing to consistently chant the mantra: "I don't know". This humility provides the sloth investor with an advantage over investors who think they can predict the future – i.e. which stock, sector or country will perform well. The simple truth is that it is very difficult to acquire such knowledge.

Humbly aware of this fact, the sloth investor simply purchases a global index fund tracker/ETF that seeks to track as much of the entire world's stock markets. Yes, some countries' stock markets will outstrip the performance of others, but, due to the absence of a crystal ball, there's no way of knowing ahead of time which countries these will be. This is why sloth investors ensure that they have exposure to developed markets and emerging markets.

In 2010, AQR Capital Management, an asset management firm, released a research paper that strongly advocates for such global diversification. In the paper, they state:

> "International diversification might not protect you from terrible days, months, or even years, but over longer horizons (which should be more important to investors) where underlying economic growth matters more to returns than short-lived panics, it protects you quite well… diversification protects investors against the adverse effects of holding concentrated positions in countries with poor long-term economic performance.
> Let us not diminish the benefits of this protection.
> In a nutshell, international diversification works on a portfolio. Ignoring it is quite simply imprudent."[47]

---

47 'International Diversification Works (Eventually)' by Clifford S. Asness, Roni Israelov and John M Liew (March 3, 2010). Available at SSRN – [ssrn.com/abstract=1564186].

In a similar vein, Daniel Crosby, author of *The Behavioral Investor*, states:

> "Diversification is likewise rooted in an ethos of, 'you can't be sure of anything so buy everything' and is proof that conceding to uncertainty does not have to mean compromising returns."[48]

What's the Difference Between Developed Markets and Emerging Markets?

A developed market quite simply represents a country that possesses an advanced economy, a reasonably high standard of living and well-developed infrastructure. The majority of developed markets are in North America, Western Europe and Australasia.

Emerging markets contain countries that are experiencing rapid economic growth, but have yet to develop high household incomes and mature infrastructure. Moreover, emerging markets are typically subject to a significant degree of political and economic stability. The size of emerging markets is dwarfed by the immense size of developed markets. However, the tremendous growth potential that they represent should not be underestimated.

Give Yourself Exposure to Developed and Emerging Markets

Owning a stake in all of the world's stock markets (or as many as you can) is a rationally informed choice, providing

---

48 Crosby, Daniel, *The Behavioral Investor* (1st ed.); (Harriman House, 2018).

you with a great chance of success. Please don't just take my word for it, though. A globally diversified approach to investing is the recommendation of numerous esteemed financial writers.

In an online interview with investment firm Rebalance, Burton Malkiel, author of the investment classic, *A Random Walk Down Wall Street*, states:

> "You want stocks that are broadly diversified internationally... and that would include the emerging markets of the world, where we are getting most of the growth... So what you want to do is to be broadly diversified."[49]

The data supports Malkiel's case for a globally diversified stock portfolio. If we take a look at the data for the top-performing global stock markets for the period 2008 to 2022 (tables 1 and 2), we can see that a wide range of countries topped the leader board.

---

49 'Own Stock Markets, Not Stocks' by Burt Malkiel. Published on *Rebalance* on 17th January 2014) – [rebalance360.com/stock-markets-stocks].

Table 1: The top-performing *developed* stock market from 2009 to 2022.[50]

2009	2010	2011	2012	2013
Norway: 87.07%	Sweden: 34.81%	Ireland: 11.37%	Belgium: 36.08%	Finland: 41.59%
2014	**2015**	**2016**	**2017**	**2018**
Israel: 20.09%	Denmark: 24.41%	Canada: 25.49%	Austria: 58.96%	New Zealand: 3.49%
2019	**2020**	**2021**	**2022**	
New Zealand: 38.83%	Denmark: 44.36%	Austria: 42.25%	Portugal 1.05%	

Table 2: The top-performing *emerging* stock market from 2009 to 2022.[51]

2009	2010	2011	2012	2013
Indonesia: 127.63%	China: 62.63%	Qatar: 8.23%	Turkey: 64.87%	UAE: 90.02%
2014	**2015**	**2016**	**2017**	**2018**
Indonesia: 27.21%	Hungary: 36.31%	Peru: 55.61%	Poland: 55.31%	China: 54.33%
2019	**2020**	**2021**	**2022**	
Greece: 43.17%	South Korea: 45.21%	Czech Republic: 58.13%	Turkey: 91.16%	

---

50 Source: MSCI Country Indexes – [msci.com]. Data retrieved on 4th July 2023.
51 Source: MSCI Country Indexes – [msci.com]. Data retrieved on 4th July 2023.

There are numerous takeaways that we can glean from Table 1 and Table 2. Firstly, eagle-eyed readers will spot the noticeable absence of both the American and British stock markets in Table 1. This should present sober reading for investors in these countries with an over exposure (a home bias) to their domestic stock market.

Table 3: The performance of the S&P 500 from 2008 to 2022.[52]

2008	2009	2010	2011	2012
-37.00%	26.46%	15.06%	2.11%	16.00%
2013	**2014**	**2015**	**2016**	**2017**
32.39%	13.69%	1.38%	11.96%	21.83%
2018	**2019**	**2020**	**2021**	**2022**
-4.38%	31.49%	18.40%	28.71%	-18.11%

While the US stock market is undoubtedly the largest stock market in the world, to consider it to be the best-performing stock market is a myth. Despite the fact that the S&P 500 achieved impressive returns during the period from 2009 to 2022 (see Table 3), it's interesting to note that a range of developed markets also performed well during this time.

Sloth Investors Do Not Possess a Crystal Ball

We can also see numerous examples of impressive stock market returns in the emerging markets of the world (see

52   Source: [slickcharts.com].

Table 2). However, we need to remember that none of us possess a crystal ball. For instance, who could have foreseen the stellar returns of the Indonesian stock market in 2009? In addition, with a return of just over 87%, the Norwegian stock market (see data for developed markets in Table 1) also had a particularly good year in 2009.

It certainly would have been tempting for investors back then to perhaps 'over allocate' their investment funds towards these specific countries. After all, with such stellar returns in 2009, it's only natural that some investors in 2010 may have felt inclined to piggyback on the success of these countries' impressive returns in the previous year. Pursuing this line of thinking further, it's not too difficult to envisage how some investors may have been tempted to commit a significant proportion of their investment funds towards emerging markets. After all, the returns of the Indonesian stock market in 2009, the Turkish stock market in 2012 and the returns of the UAE stock market the following year were all particularly impressive.

Contrary to this approach, though, it's important to remember that there is no guarantee of consistent investment returns from one year to the next. On this point, Andrew Hallam, author of *Millionaire Expat – How to Build Wealth Living Overseas*, states:

> "It's better to spread your risk and go with a global
> stock market index... with it, you'll have exposure to
> older world economies such as England, France, and
> Germany, as well as younger, fast-growing economies
> like China, India, Brazil, and Thailand... Investors with

> portfolios tilted heavily toward emerging markets (e.g.
> India, Brazil, China) take massive global capitalization
> risk. Emerging markets make up roughly 13% of global
> market value. So it makes little sense for most investors
> to have more than 13% of their portfolio in emerging
> market stocks."[53]

An allocation to emerging markets is undoubtedly important, but it's important to stress again that the sloth investor invests proportionally, based on the market capitalisation of the global stock market. So, emerging markets currently represent around 10 to 15% of the global stock market, which means that a sloth investor should allocate around 10 to 15% of their equity portfolio to emerging markets.

The Misfortunes of 'Patriotic Pete' – a Case Study in Home Bias

The decade from 2000 to 2009 was a disappointing period for the US stock market. Therefore, American investors with a significant home bias would have seen their portfolio achieve lacklustre returns. However, a more broadly diversified portfolio would have performed better.

It's worth diving a little deeper to explore the case for a portfolio containing a significant tilt towards international diversification.

---

53 Hallam, Andrew, *Millionaire Expat: How to Build Wealth Living Overseas* (2nd ed.), (Wiley: 2018).

It's Business as Usual, Right? Show Me the Money!

Imagine that you're an American investor in 2000, feeling confident at the turn of the century about your nation's prospects; after all, wasn't the 20th century the American century? Surely the new decade will bring with it continued prosperity, right?

Yes, you're a proud, patriotic American, which means that you wholeheartedly commit yourself to investing in an index fund that represents the American stock market. Let's call this investor 'Patriotic Pete'. Unfortunately (well, certainly for Pete, anyway), the first decade of the 21st century brought with it disappointing returns in the American stock market. In fact, for the period between January 2000 and December 2009, American investors with a home bias would have made a loss! That's right, a $10,000 dollar investment in a leading American index fund would have been valued at $9,016[54] (assuming no additional contributions by the investor). Wait just a moment, though, because you may be thinking that it was the financial crisis of 2007 to 2008 that caused much of the damage. Again, it's worth exploring the data.

Let's say Patriotic Pete had a crystal ball and he was able to foresee the financial crisis that occurred in the latter part of the first decade of the 21st century. So, let's assume that he pulled his money out of the stock market on 31st December 2006. In this case, his return would have indeed been positive, but not by much. This is because for the period between January 2000 and 31st December 2006,

---

54   All comparison data taken from [portfoliovisualiser.com]. The American index used was the 'Vanguard 500 Index Investor'.

Pete's portfolio grew at an average annual rate of just 1.03% a year, leaving him with a balance of $10,740 (assuming no additional contributions by the investor). Once you take into account the effect of inflation, you have to seriously consider whether he made any money at all.

Pete reflected on the first decade of the century and, though still a proud American, he decided not to invest any more in his nation's stock market. After several years of disappointing returns in the early part of the decade, the financial crisis of 2007 to 2008 rubbed further salt into the wounds. "That's it, I'm out," said Pete, echoing the sentiments of many other American investors at the time.

Was this a wise decision by Pete, though? Well, fortunately for Americans (that were invested), the second decade of the 21st century proved to be a much better time to be invested in the American stock market. For the period between January 1st 2010 and December 31st 2019, investors in an index fund representing the American stock market would have seen the value of their stock portfolio grow by an average of 13.40% a year, turning an initial amount of $10,000 into $67,683 (assuming no additional contributions by the investor).

Reflections on Pete's Portfolio Pain

So, there we have it, two decades of pain but for differing reasons. As he reflected on the performance of his portfolio in the first decade of the 21st century, Pete's pain stemmed from its disappointing return during this period. Then, in early 2020, Pete again felt the pain of mental anguish, but this time for different reasons. On this occasion, he reflected on the cost of not being invested and on missing out on the return of seeing his portfolio grow by an average amount of 13.40% a year.

What Could Pete Have Done Differently?

By now, I hope it's been made clear that investing in a global equity portfolio provides you with broad diversification and reduces the risk associated with overexposure to your domestic stock market. Likewise, for Pete, a broader degree of diversification would have seen an improvement in his portfolio's fortunes. Using data from portfoliovisualiser. com, we can see that emerging markets grew by an average of 9.82% during the period of 2000 to 2010. So, as discussed, even though emerging markets represent a relatively small percentage of the world's stock markets, an allocation (even if small) to them during 2000 to 2010 would have seen Pete's portfolio perform better during this period.

Now, of course, just like everyone else, Pete was not in possession of a crystal ball. How was he supposed to know in advance about the outperformance of emerging markets, relative to the performance of the American stock market during the period 2000 to 2009? The point is not to actively reorient the allocation of one's portfolio from one decade to the next. Rather, there needs to be an appreciation for the benefits of consistent, broad, global diversification. A 2019 Vanguard research paper, entitled 'Global Equity Investing: The Benefits of Diversification and Sizing Your Allocation', states:

"Another benefit of global diversification is the
opportunity to participate in whichever regional market
is outperforming… for example, while the United States
may lead over some periods, another country or region
will invariably lead at other points."[55]

Sloth Investors Show 'Home Market Humility'

Diversification in this manner is, therefore, an example of what I call 'home market humility', which is the recognition that though there may be merits to one's domestic stock market, the best approach is to engage in broad global diversification.

In a *Let's Talk ETFs* podcast interview in March 2020, Larry Swedroe, author of *What Wall Street Doesn't Want You to Know* and *Rational Investing in Irrational Times*, states:

"No one knows when these things switch regimes.
So, the best strategy is to diversify… the purpose
of diversifying is exactly that: to avoid the risk of
concentrating all of your assets… that's the mistake
Japanese investors made in 1990… because my crystal
ball is always cloudy, I want to diversify across as many
unique sources of risk as I can identify."[56]

---

55 'Global Equity Investing: The Benefits of Diversification and Sizing Your Allocation' by Brian J. Scott, CFA; Kimberly A. Stockton; Scott J. Donaldson. Vanguard Research, February 2019 – [corporate.vanguard.com/content/dam/corp/research/pdf/Global-equity-investing-The-benefits-of-diversification-and-sizing-your-allocation-US-ISGGEB_042021_Online.pdf].

56 Seeking Alpha, 2021. 'Larry Swedroe's Timeless Investing Wisdom For This (And Every Other) Market Panic' podcast. *Let's Talk ETFs*. Available at: [podcasts.apple.com/us/podcast/larry-swedroes-timeless-investing-wisdom-for-this-and/id1466669216?i=1000470172090].

Finally, Lars Kroijer, author of *Investing Demystified*, states:

> "Some books on investing involve intricate arguments
> about why certain geographical areas or sectors of the
> equity markets will outperform and provide a safe haven
> for the investor. On the contrary, the most diversified
> portfolio you can find offers the greatest protection
> against regional declines. Also, since we are simply
> saying 'buy the world', the product is very simple and
> should be super cheap. Over the long run that will
> matter greatly. The portfolio is as diversified as possible
> and each dollar invested in the market is presumed
> equally clever, consistent with what a rational investor
> believes. Since we are simply saying 'buying the market'
> as broadly as we can, it's a very simple portfolio to
> construct and thus very cheap. We don't have to pay
> anyone to be smart about beating the market. Over
> time the cost-benefit can make a huge difference.
> Don't ignore that. This kind of broad-based portfolio
> is now available to most investors whereas only a
> couple of decades ago it was not. Take advantage of this
> development to buy broader-based products."[57]

Buying index trackers/ETFs to spread their stock investments
over multiple stocks, sectors and nation-states provides the
necessary diversification for a sloth investor. Pursuing such
an investment strategy by investing in a low-fee, globally
diversified index tracker/ETF is straightforward. Indeed, the
providers of these index trackers/ETFs, such as Vanguard

---

57 Kroijer, Lars, *Investing Demystified: How to Invest Without Specu-
     lation and Sleepless Nights*, (2nd ed), (FT Publishing International,
     2017).

and iShares, make it easy to see how each of their funds is allocated to specific regions, sectors and stocks. In Chapter 8, I provide you with these fund options.

A Collector's Mentality

As a father, I never cease to be amazed by the varied items that my children are keen to collect. My daughter takes great pride in collecting seashells whenever she visits the beach. My son has a particular penchant for rocks and for rare coins.

This mentality of collecting items is not limited to children though. My late mother was consistently keen to collect novelty mugs and, in the 1990s, she seemed hellbent on collecting 'Hard Rock Cafe' shirts from around the world. So, what has this got to do with investing, I hear you say? Well, I would like to begin to bring this section on 'Owning the World' to an end by urging you to develop a collector's mentality for the finest businesses from around the world.

Investing in a low-fee, globally diversified ETF enables you to collect and, indeed, become a part owner of thousands of businesses from around the world. Something that I'm always struck by, with regards to the fanatical collectors that I know, is the ability of these people to continually focus on growing their collection (whether this be stamps, action figures or coins) instead of focusing on the present worth or net value of these items.

Likewise, as a sloth investor, I encourage you to cultivate the habit of continually investing in a broad, globally diversified manner, thereby ensuring that you grow your own collection of the world's best businesses. As I remarked upon earlier, low-fee, globally diversified index funds/ETFs were not available to my parents' generation when they were young. I encourage you to embrace their contemporary availability as an opportunity to benefit from the industry and innovation of a variety of great businesses from around the world.

Apart from Stocks, What Does Mr Sloth Collect?

My wife, Justine, affectionately known as 'Mrs Sloth', occasionally teases me for my collection of white T-shirts. Yes, that's right. White T-shirts. So, why does Mr Sloth possess a collection of white T-shirts? The reason is quite simple. Simplicity! The author of this book has what you might term a 'no-frills' fashion sense, meaning that a simple white T-shirt (I have multiple kinds) has become a staple of my wardrobe.

Some readers may recollect that the late Steve Jobs, the founder of Apple, engaged in a similar approach with his wardrobe. Despite being a millionaire many times over, Jobs possessed a particular preference for blue jeans and a black turtleneck T-shirt. If you check out his iPhone product presentations on YouTube, it'll be easy for you to identify the trademark garments that made him the world's most recognisable CEO. Walter Isaacson, the author of the authorised biography of Steve Jobs, had this to say on the late Apple CEO's wardrobe habit:

> "He (Jobs) also came to like the idea of having a uniform for himself, both because of its daily convenience (the rationale he claimed) and its ability to convey a signature style."[58]

58　Isaacson, Walter, *Steve Jobs*, (Simon & Schuster: 2015).

It's perhaps fitting (no pun intended) that I devote the very last component of this section on 'Owning the World' to the garments customarily worn by Steve Jobs. At the current time of writing, Apple frequently holds the largest position in most low-fee, globally diversified index funds/ETFs, which is the key portfolio holding that the Sloth Investor advocates for investors, young and old.

Acknowledging Decision Fatigue and Information Overload

Let's now dig a little deeper into the rationale for Jobs' clothing of choice. A chief reason for Jobs' 'uniform' of blue jeans and a black turtleneck T-shirt was to avoid decision fatigue. Or, to put another way, it was to reduce information overload. The reason why the concepts of 'decision fatigue' and 'information overload' are worth discussing here is because of their relevance to the approach to investing that I have advocated throughout this section of the book, which is an approach that fundamentally underpins my investing philosophy.

Quite simply, by investing in a low-fee, globally diversified index fund/ETF, you significantly reduce the potential for information overload to unduly influence the investment decisions that you take. Why? Well, let's consider the alternative route. If you choose to embrace the notion that you can skilfully assemble a selection of businesses, this then comes with a resultant consequence. The consequence is that you will have to continually monitor the operations of these businesses. Are they continuing to grow revenues? Are they staying ahead of their business rivals? Is there plenty of room for the business to grow into the future? As a shareholder of these companies, these are just a few of the questions that you must continually seek to assess. Again, let's touch upon the concept of 'advantage' that I referred to earlier on in this section. What advantage will you possess in terms of being able to continually assess (in an accurate way) the business operations of the select group of companies that you have chosen to invest in? There is an abundance of information available to contemporary investors. However, how confident are you that you possess the necessary ability to prioritise some information over others?

A Low-Fee, Globally Diversified Portfolio – the Simple Approach to Investing

Alternatively, to avoid information overload, you can choose to adhere to the sloth investor's first bedrock principle of *simplicity* by simply buying a low-fee, globally diversified equity index fund/ETF on a consistent basis, through good times and bad (known as 'dollar cost averaging').

Investing in this manner takes the guesswork out of investing and ensures that you sleep better at night, by not having to fret and worry about the complex business operations of a select group of companies. Instead, you can lay your head down on the pillow safe in the knowledge that you simply own the world. Sweet dreams are made of this!

Mr Sloth's Summary:

- It's tempting to commit a significant portion of your hard-earned income to investments in the companies of your home country. After all, these may very well be the companies that you use on a daily basis. However, just because you're familiar with them doesn't mean that they'll make great, long-term investments. Instead, ensure that you invest in a global index fund/ETF tracker that is allocated according to the percentage representations of the countries that constitute the global stock market.
- A low-fee, globally diversified index fund/ETF provides you with exposure to stocks, sectors and nation-states.
- Embrace investing in a globally diversified manner as an opportunity to benefit from the great global businesses of the world. It will enable you to reduce information overload, thereby allowing you to sleep better at night. Zzz...

Time

"The big money is not in the buying and selling,
but in the waiting."

Charlie Munger

Prioritise Funds You Need for the Short Term

Let's begin this section on the fourth bedrock principle of the sloth investor, time, with an important disclaimer. Money that you need within the next five years *should not* be invested in the stock market. The sloth investor invests with a multi-decade time horizon and this should be paramount in your thinking.

Over the short term, there will inevitably be occasions when money may be needed for such things as university fees, an overseas trip, a wedding or perhaps the purchase of a second-hand car (naturally, though, such expenditures will be dependent upon factors like your age and personal circumstances).

The long-term, positive, upwards movement of the stock market has been remarkable to observe. Over the short term, though, the performance of the stock market can be less predictable. Therefore, it's important that you preserve any money that you are certain to require within a five-year time period.

Time Is on Your Side

It is my fundamental belief that an appreciation of the historical returns of the stock market is critical to one's success as an investor. Acknowledging and acting upon an understanding of the long-term historical returns of the stock market provides investors with a solid underpinning for success.

History > Hysteria

The long-term trend of the stock market is for it to rise. The author of this book reduces risk by investing in an ETF that tracks an index containing a diversified, global portfolio of stocks.

The MSCI ACWI Index represents the performance of stocks across twenty-three developed countries and twenty-four emerging markets. For the time period between 31st December 1987 to 31st May 2023, the average annual return of this index has been 7.85%.[59]

As the most prominent stock market in the world, there is even more data available for the US stock market. In his book, *Stocks for the Long Run*, Jeremy Siegel, Professor of Finance at the Wharton School of the University of Pennsylvania in Philadelphia, states that the average annual return of the US stock market between 1802 and 2012 was 8.1%.[60]

Depending on which source you use, whether this is a book, podcast or financial news channel, you're always likely to take note of a 7 to 10% figure for the average annual

---

59   Source: [msci.com].
60   Siegel, J., *Stocks for the Long Run: The Definitive Guide to Financial Market Returns & Long-Term Investment Strategies* (5th ed.), (Mc-Graw Hill: 2014).

return of the stock market. Though these returns have been remarkably consistent throughout history, it's important to note the wide variability of calendar year returns.

For example, in one year, the index may return 30%, the next year it could return 2% and the following year could see a negative return. Table 4 shows the calendar year returns for the MSCI ACWI Index from 2006 to 2022. Interestingly, you'll note that an annual return figure of between 7 to 10% only occurred once during this time period (8.48% in 2016).

Table 4: The annual performance (%) of the MSCI ACWI IMI Index from 2006 to 2022.[61]

Year	MSCI ACWI (global equity index)
2022	-17.96
2021	19.04
2020	16.82
2019	27.30
2018	-8.93
2017	24.62
2016	8.48
2015	-1.84
2014	4.71
2013	23.44
2012	16.80
2011	-6.86
2010	13.21
2009	35.41

61   Source: [msci.com].

2008	-42.19
2007	12.18
2006	21.53

Historically, global equity investors have seen positive annual returns occurring around 70 to 75% of the time with negative annual returns occurring 25 to 30% of the time.

The data from Table 4 clearly demonstrates this, as the period from 2006 to 2022 showed positive returns in the MSCI ACWI (global equity index) 71% of the time and negative returns 29% of the time, with twelve of the seventeen years from 2006 to 2022 posting a positive return and five of the sixteen years posting a negative return.

In Table 5, you will see the annual performance data for the S&P 500 stretching all the way back for almost a century, from 1926 to 2022. Just like the data for the MSCI ACWI Index, the historical data for the S&P 500 reaffirms the fact that market returns are more frequently positive than negative. You'll note that a positive annual return occurred in seventy-one out of ninety-seven years – or 73% of the time – meaning that a negative annual return occurred in twenty-six of these years – or 27% of the time.

The data for the S&P 500 does an amazing job of showing the wide variability of annual returns. It's fascinating to observe that an annual return figure of between 7 to 10% only occurred once during this time period (7.62% in 1992). Yes, that's right, just once in ninety-seven years!

Don't Expect Average!

Table 5: Annual performance of the S&P 500 from 1926 to 2022 (dividends reinvested).[62]

Year	Return	Year	Return	Year	Return	Year	Return	Year	Return
1926	11.62	1945	36.44	1964	16.48	1983	22.56	2002	-22.10
1927	37.49	1946	-8.07	1965	12.45	1984	6.27	2003	28.68
1928	43.61	1947	5.71	1966	-10.06	1985	31.73	2004	10.88
1929	-8.42	1948	5.50	1967	23.98	1986	18.67	2005	4.91
1930	-24.90	1949	18.79	1968	11.06	1987	5.25	2006	15.79
1931	-43.34	1950	31.71	1969	-8.50	1988	16.61	2007	5.49
1932	-8.19	1951	24.02	1970	4.01	1989	31.69	2008	-37.00
1933	53.99	1952	18.37	1971	14.31	1990	-3.10	2009	26.46
1934	-1.44	1953	-0.99	1972	18.98	1991	30.47	2010	15.06
1935	47.67	1954	52.62	1973	-14.66	1992	7.62	2011	2.11
1936	33.92	1955	31.56	1974	-26.47	1993	10.08	2012	16.00
1937	-35.03	1956	6.56	1975	37.20	1994	1.32	2013	32.39
1938	31.12	1957	-10.78	1976	23.84	1995	37.58	2014	13.69
1939	-0.41	1958	43.36	1977	-7.18	1996	22.96	2015	1.38
1940	-9.78	1959	11.96	1978	6.56	1997	33.36	2016	11.96
1941	-11.59	1960	0.47	1979	18.44	1998	28.58	2017	21.83
1942	20.34	1961	26.89	1980	32.42	1999	21.04	2018	-4.38
1943	25.90	1962	-8.73	1981	-4.91	2000	-9.10	2019	31.49
1944	19.75	1963	22.80	1982	21.55	2001	-11.89	2020	18.40
								2021	28.71
								2022	-18.11

---

62   Source: [slickcharts.com].

Place Your Trust in the Steady Staircase!

It's undeniable that the stock market rises more than it falls. Despite this, it's important to acknowledge that when the market crashes, it moves down like an elevator. In contrast, when it rises again, it gradually moves upwards like a steady staircase. The gradual historic upwards trajectory of the stock market has truly been a sight to behold.

Historically, the returns of the world's largest stock market, the US stock market, are positive in roughly three out of every four years. Furthermore, if we look at a five-year period, your chance of obtaining a positive return on your investment is almost 90%. Finally, if we zoom out to twenty years, the US stock market has shown positive returns over all twenty-year periods historically.[63]

In spite of this, there are still some that express scepticism about this form of investing one's capital. Media hysteria concerning the stock market is unquestionably a key reason for such scepticism.

Should You Watch Financial News?

Let's explore why investing in the stock market is often associated with such high levels of hysteria. Crucially, it's important to recognise the business model of financial news channels.

One of the key aims of such channels is to increase viewership. The reason for this is simple. More viewers = increased revenue from advertising. How can financial news

---

63   Fisher, Ken, *The Little Book of Market Myths: How to Profit by Avoiding the Investing Mistakes Everyone Else Makes* (1st ed.); (Wiley: 2013).

channels attract viewers? They attract viewers by creating content that is designed to elicit an emotional reaction from you. Here's a few examples:

> "Stay tuned for our next market forecast. Things could be about to get bumpy."

> "You won't want to miss what this leading analyst has to say about the next market drop."

Yes, it's beyond doubt that reporting in this way will certainly give cause for concern to some people, but instead of succumbing to such utterances, a sloth investor merely changes the channel or simply doesn't watch the financial news channels at all. This is because, unlike many investors, who sadly succumb to the hysterical headlines that characterise the financial media, a sloth investor maintains a steadfast commitment to remaining invested at all times.

Quite simply, a sloth investor stays the course! Using historical data as their guide, sloth investors think in a rational manner, ensuring that their view of the stock market is shaped by history and *not* the hysteria of the financial and mainstream media.

Don't Allow the News to Affect Your Approach to Investing

One of the most influential books that I have ever read is the late Hans Rosling's *Factfulness*.[64] In this landmark, insightful

---

64 Rosling, H., Rönnlund, A. R., & Rosling, O., *Factfulness: Ten Reasons We're Wrong About the World – and Why Things Are Better Than You Think* (Flatiron Books, 2018).

book, Rosling explores the disproportionate coverage given to negative news in the mainstream media. Rosling notes how stories that refer to gradual improvements rarely make the front page.

In this regard, the parallels to investing are striking. Switch on a financial news channel or read an investment-themed article in a broadsheet paper and invariably you'll learn that the *modus operandi* of these media channels is to engage in hysterical, sensationalist-laden reportage. A more responsible course of action for these media outlets would be to outline to their audience the merits of committing to a long-term view of the stock market.

Circling back to Rosling's point about the disproportionate coverage given to negative news, there have been innumerable geopolitical news stories over the last sixty years that could have 'spooked' investors, causing them to exit the stock market, due to the fear of impending doom.

Table 6 provides a summary of some of the key political moments of the past six decades. It cannot be denied that geopolitical events can certainly play havoc with the markets. Though some investors may have succumbed to mental weakness, those that were able to resist the urge to sell during these periods would have been rewarded for their patience. The crucial lesson to investors is to remain patient and to 'ride out' any sustained periods of volatility caused by these events.

Table 6: A summary of key geopolitical events from 1960 to 2022.

1960s	1970s
1962: Cuban Missile Crisis 1963: JFK assassinated 1965: US combat troops arrive in Vietnam 1967: Arab-Israeli War 1968: MLK & Bobby Kennedy assassinated	1971: Indo-Pakistani War 1972: Watergate scandal 1973: Oil crisis 1974: President Nixon resigns 1979: Soviet-Afghan War begins
1980s	**1990s**
1980: Iran-Iraq War begins 1981: Brixton riots in the UK 1982: Falklands War 1986: Chernobyl disaster 1987: Black Monday – market crash 1989: Tokyo stock market crash	1990: Gulf War begins 1991: UK recession 1997: Asia financial crisis
2000s	**2010-2019**
2000: Burst of the dot.com bubble 2001: 9/11 2001: Afghanistan War begins 2003: Invasion of Iraq, SARS 2004: Train bombing in Madrid 2005: Public transport bombing in London 2006: Hurricane Katrina 2008: Global financial crisis	2011: Japanese tsunami, London riots 2012: Greek government debt crisis 2014: Conflict in Crimea & Ukraine, Ebola outbreak 2015-2016: Chinese stock market turbulence 2016: Brexit vote 2017: Donald Trump is inaugurated 2019: Covid-19 begins

Wall Street (Investing > Trading)

For many of us, our first experience of the stock market comes from news footage of the trading floor of the New York Stock Exchange. It's in this location that we're presented with the familiar cast of characters that the mainstream media uses to depict the stock market. The principal cast member? The Wall Street trader. As a sloth investor, you must recognise that the time period the Wall Street trader values will be different to the time period that you should value. This is because Wall Street traders are incentivised to deliver returns over short periods.

The application of time, the fourth bedrock principle of a sloth investor, helps us to define the difference between trading and investing. Simply, a trading mindset relies upon getting in and out of the stock at precise times. On the other hand, like Warren Buffett, a sloth investor recognises that 'time in the market beats timing the market'.

Frequent trading and market timing leads to poor performance. You, the individual investor, will achieve much greater success by adhering to a long-term horizon.

A Parallel Universe

When you see footage of the trading floor at the New York Stock Exchange, you have to remember that they are operating in a parallel universe to you, the sloth investor. Often, you may observe that these traders, with their customary blue blazer and state-of-the-art electronic device, look agitated. Why is this? Well, remember, to the NYSE trader, or any trader for that matter, the 'quick buck' is everything. Patience is anathema to them. However, for you, the sloth investor, patience is your trump card.

It's unfortunate that for so many people, their only experience of the stock market comes during those occasional snapshots of life on the trading floor of the New York Stock Exchange. Is it any wonder that potential investors are deterred from investing by the sight of these stressed traders? However, you must not allow your perception of the stock market to be shaped by such images. Remember, the trader's time horizon defines their erratic behaviour.

Patience (Patience > Impatience)

As we dive ever deeper into the 21st century, it's useful to reflect upon the monumental ways that technology has affected our lives in the last few decades. I would argue that humans have become spoiled by our increasingly 'frictionless' society. In the event that you are unfamiliar with this term, 'frictionless' refers to the ability to achieve something with little difficulty or, in other words, to be effortless. Netflix and Amazon are undoubtedly two of the companies that have been leading the way in this brave new 'frictionless' world. Ronny Chieng, a Malaysian comedian, perfectly encapsulated the way that Amazon has accelerated our desire for frictionless commerce, when, in a Netflix special, he hilariously asserted:

> "We need it, Prime. We need Prime harder, faster, stronger... Faster Prime! Prime now! Prime Now! Two-

> hour delivery! Prime Now! Give it to me now! When I
> press 'buy', put the item in my hand now!"[65]

Naturally, we laugh at the thought of such a luxuriant life cycle, but as Kevin Kelly, author of *The Inevitable: Understanding the 12 Technological Forces That Will Shape Our Future*, writes: "Our appetite for the instant is insatiable."[66]

Conditioned for Immediate Gratification?

So, what does our frictionless society have to do with investing? Why is it such a problem that the conveniences of contemporary society (Netflix, Amazon, Google, Uber et al.) have conditioned so many of us to immediate gratification?

Well, I would argue that our 'need for speed' is causing a significant number of people to become increasingly impatient. The resultant effect is that many of these individuals are not willing to commit the time necessary to become investors. In his book, *The Little Book of Behavioral Investing,* author James Montier writes:

> "Investors today appear to have chronic attention
> hyperactivity disorder (ADHD) when it comes to their
> portfolio."[67]

---

65 *Ronny Chieng: Asian Comedian Destroys America.* Retrieved from [www.netflix.com].

66 Kelly, Kevin, *The Inevitable: Understanding the 12 Technological Forces That Will Shape Our Future* (Reprint ed.); (Penguin Books, 2016).

67 Montier, James, *The Little Book of Behavioral Investing: How Not to Be Your Own Worst Enemy* (1st ed.); (Wiley, 2010).

Earlier I spoke about how I wrote a significant amount of this book during the initial period of Covid-19. Interestingly, during this period, the media reported on a noticeable escalation in the number of people trading stocks. By now, you know that this book advocates *investing* instead of *trading* one's money.

Trading stocks is the 'short distance', 'sprint-like', dangerous approach to allocating one's money. Remember, there's no need for you to be in a rush, particularly if you have multiple decades ahead of you. In his insightful book, *In Praise of Slowness*, author Carl Honore states:

> "Why are we always in such a rush?... In these early years of the twenty-first century, everything and everyone is under pressure to go faster... But now the time has come to challenge our obsession with doing everything more quickly. Speed is not always the best policy. Evolution works on the principle of survival of the fittest, not the fastest."[68]

I discussed the concept of patience when referring to Wall Street traders earlier on. However, because I consider it to be such a critical ingredient for investing success, I believe the concept of patience now warrants further discussion.

First of all, please take a moment to reflect and think about the achievements in your life. How many of those achievements have been attained over a short time period? Driving a car, riding a bike, mastering a musical instrument

---

68   Honore, Carl, *In Praise of Slowness: Challenging the Cult of Speed*, (HarperOne: 2005).

– you name it, invariably these skills are typically acquired over a long time duration. It's typically the case that the short-term application of effort doesn't immediately yield positive results. Instead, sustained effort, over a longer time horizon, produces the results that you desire.

I have friends that have excitedly purchased gym membership at the beginning of a new year, with the expectation that they will quickly develop a sleeker, more physically toned appearance. However, after several weeks, some of these friends gave up, due to the fact that they had not achieved the results that they had desired.

Conversely, I have other friends that did not give up and were willing to persevere. The crucial distinction between these two sets of friends? Time horizon. My friends that struggled to persist with their gym work failed to adhere to a long time horizon in their quest to become fitter. In other words, they were impatient. My friends that 'stuck it out', who persevered, even when the results seemed unnoticeable in the short term, were patient. They realised that positive results don't come overnight. It takes time to yield positive achievements.

We can make similar connections to dieting. Although I won't name them, for fear of being cast out as a black sheep, there are members of my family that have failed to benefit from the potential positive effects of a diet. Why was this? Well, you've guessed it, a short time horizon. Just like a short-term commitment to gym work is unlikely to yield that much progress, a failure to commit to a diet over a long-term time horizon is likely to generate similar results.

A Jedi of Patience

What does visiting the gym and dieting have to do with investing? Are these pursuits perhaps analogous to investing? Yes, they are. By adhering to a long-term time horizon, the sloth investor is a jedi of patience. A sloth investor realises that success as an investor doesn't occur overnight, it may not even appear after a year.

A sloth investor invests over a multi-decade time horizon. A sloth investor recognises that behaviour like this is significantly more likely to lead to positive outcomes. Remember, 0.01% of investing is about buying and 99.99% is about waiting. Do you have the mindset to sit and be patient? On this need to be patient and this sloth-like ability to be inactive, Brian Portnoy, author of *The Geometry of Wealth*, states:

> "One of the greatest skills in investing is patience, the
> Stoic ability to do nothing deliberately. In our money
> lives and well beyond, those who have mastered the art
> of delayed gratification are more likely to excel."[69]

Don't Become a Slave to the Calendar (Blindfold Wearing > Calendar Gazing)

Standard measures are great. They provide us with a universal mathematical language that can be understood by people around the world.

It's common in the investment world for people to use the calendar to describe the performance of a particular fund.

---

69   Portnoy, Brian, *The Geometry of Wealth: How To Shape a Life of Money and Meaning*. (Harriman House: 2018).

It's the investing world's standard measure of performance. What was the performance last year? This is a question you may hear on financial news channels or read in the financial section of broadsheet newspapers.

Remember, over a short-term basis, the behaviour of the stock market can be erratic. The stock market could move steadily up (which it does a significant amount of the time) or it could move down. For this reason, a sloth investor wears two items on their head: a blindfold and a set of ear muffs. These two items enable the sloth investor to remain impervious to the return of one specific calendar year in the stock market. This is because a sloth investor understands the importance of rigidly sticking to a multi-decade time horizon. Yes, there are years when the stock market may fall, but when viewed through the rear mirror of a multi-decade vantage point, these dips appear like nothing but a small blip.

In an article for *Internaxx* titled, 'The Biggest Challenge That Investors Face Now!', Andrew Hallam states:

> "Nor should investors focus on a single year's return. In fact, they shouldn't pay attention to a single decade either. Your investment duration, after all, spans beyond your working lifetime. It spans as long as you'll be living."[70]

Similarly, in a September 2015 article entitled, 'Tyranny of the Calendar', Morgan Housel states:

---

70   'The Biggest Challenge That Investors Face Now!' by Andrew Hallam (May 2019) – [swissquote.lu/international-investing/wealth-building/biggest-challenge-investors-face-these-uncertain-times?ref=andrewhallam.com].

> "Performance has to be measured, and measures need
> a yardstick, however arbitrary... Investing, though, is
> personal. All that matters is performance between today
> and your end goal, not the individual years in between."[71]

Always Be Invested > Withdraw Everything at Retirement

There's often a common misconception that, upon retirement, an individual should sell everything in their investment portfolio and then live off the proceeds. The thinking behind such an approach is flawed. Let's say you've invested like a sloth for multiple decades and you reach the age of sixty and you're able to retire.

Withdrawing everything may do wonders for your ego. The sudden addition of a nice, hefty amount of cash in your bank account undoubtedly makes you feel great. Despite this, before you rush to click on the 'sell all' option within your investing account, you need to consider whether you've thought about the opportunity cost of not being invested.

So, you retire at age sixty and let's say you live for another thirty years. The opportunity cost of not remaining invested for those thirty years would be tremendous. Though you may feel content with the amount you've accrued in your investment account, just consider, for a moment, how much more you could grow your wealth by if you remained invested at all times. Your investment duration should extend beyond

---

71 'Tyranny of the Calendar' by Morgan Housel. Published on The Motley Fool on 29th September 2015 – [fool.com/investing/general/2015/09/29/the-tyranny-of-the-calendar.aspx].

your working life. Simply, you should remain invested for as long as you live.

Naturally, at this point, some sensible questions you may ask are: What happens if there's a stock market crash as I approach retirement? What happens if there's a stock market crash in my early years of retirement?

These are excellent questions to ask. Who wants to suffer from a stock market decline that could strip as much as 40% from the overall value of your portfolio? Of course, no one does. So, what can you do? This is where bonds can play an important role in your portfolio. If you haven't done so already, please make sure that you read the section of the book on bonds in the chapter entitled, 'Considerations for Your Sloth Portfolio'.

Decades > Days

Interestingly, I am writing this section on 'Time' during the midst of a volatile time for the stock market. The reason? Coronavirus. During this week, in March 2020, stock markets around the world have been rapidly falling. Concerns about the economic impact of the virus, such as falling productivity and weaker consumer spending, have caused plunging prices. Is it fun to see the value of your portfolio dip by 10 to 12% in a single week? Of course not. However, the deployment of perspective is important. This is because, at times such as this, it's important to remember that the sloth investor invests for decades, not days. A sloth investor is a long-term investor.

The performance of the stock market over a five-day

period should be of little consequence to someone who adopts a multi-decade time horizon. Okay, so let's say the market suffers from a prolonged period of volatility longer than five days. What if volatility lasts for six months? Again, that's a very short time horizon. Don't concern yourself with the stock market's performance over six months, you should be more concerned with its performance over 600 months (if you're not mathematically inclined, that's fifty years).

Remember, you're investing for the long run. Simply put, if you are saving for retirement and you have a time horizon greater than a decade, it is imperative that you overcome the temptation to fret and concern yourself with the volatility that is a natural part of the terrain for an investor.

Invariably, during these periodic bouts of volatility, it may be that you read a news article or watch a news segment full of sensationalistic fervour concerning the day's events on Wall Street. No doubt you'll catch a glimpse of the anxiety-laden expressions and furrowed brows of an assortment of Wall Street traders. It's worth repeating what I stated earlier. Wall Street traders are incentivised to deliver returns over short periods.

What's the final word in their job title? Trader. When you catch sight of their flustered faces and their frantic movements on the trading room floor, it is critical that you remember the advantage that you have over them – time. These Wall Street traders are fully cognizant of the fact that, as traders, they will be judged on their short-term performance. Their goal, as I mentioned before, is the 'quick buck'. Your goal is your long-term future. Don't lose sight of that.

Investing > Gambling

A common criticism of investing often uttered by the layperson is that investing is nothing more than a form of gambling. It is important to note, though, that any comparison between investing and gambling is misjudged, as it fails to take into account the key dimension of time.

You will note that at the beginning of this section on time, I stated that money that you need within the next five years should *not* be invested in the stock market. This is because the short-term performance of the stock market, particularly over, say, a one-year period can be less predictable. So, I would argue and, indeed, humbly admit that investing money that you will need twelve months later certainly is a form of gambling. However, by looking at the long-term, multi-decade returns of the stock market, we can see that the returns are more consistently, overwhelmingly positive than if one were to simply look at returns over a one-year period only. Therefore, I would argue that investing money that you won't need for at least another decade, while not entirely without risk, carries with it less similarity to gambling.

So, essentially, when you enter a casino, the house is always expected to win over the long run on average. However, when it comes to investing, the longer you remain invested, the more likely it is that the eventual outcome will be positive.

If any form of capital allocation were to provide us with a greater resemblance to gambling, I would argue that it is trading. Remember: the sloth investor *does not* trade, the sloth investor *invests*.

Mr Sloth's Summary:

- Money that you need within the next five years should *not* be invested in the stock market.

- Although an average annual return of 7 to 10% for the stock market has been remarkably consistent throughout history, it's important to note the wide variability of calendar year returns. For example, if you were to handpick ten random calendar year returns of the S&P 500, it's unlikely that many of the years (perhaps, if any) would have produced a calendar year return in the range of 7 to 10%. The data from this chapter, presented in Table 5, bears this out.

- The gradual historic upwards trajectory of the stock market has truly been a sight to behold. It's important to remember that when the market crashes, it moves down like an elevator. In contrast, when it rises again, it gradually moves upwards, like a steady staircase.

- Our contemporary conveniences (Amazon, Netflix, Uber et al.) have conditioned many to immediate gratification. However, the danger of such 'frictionless' experiences is that they compel us to become accustomed to achieving outcomes within a short time frame, perhaps, even, to become impatient. Remember, though, that the greatest fruits of investing belong to the patient.

- Don't let disproportionate coverage allocated to 'negative' news affect your investing time frame.

- Your investment duration should extend beyond your working life. Put simply, you should remain invested for as long as you live.

Headstrong

"He who conquers himself is the mightiest warrior."

Confucius

"In investing, emotional intelligence trumps financial intelligence."

Brian Portnoy, *The Geometry of Wealth*

Look in the Mirror!

Okay, we've finally reached the last bedrock principle of Mr Sloth: the ability to be headstrong. While this isn't a case of leaving the best to last, it certainly is, in my opinion, a case of leaving the most important to last. This is because the individual investor doesn't need to look far to encounter what is likely to be the biggest obstacle to their success as an investor. Yes, quite simply, take a look in the mirror and you'll find it. You can put such principles as low fees, owning the world and a long time horizon to the side for now, because unless you're able to control yourself, to obtain mastery over your emotions, the performance of your portfolio will wither into insignificance. You are the biggest obstacle to your investing success!

Once Upon a Time on Wall Street

One of the perks of being a sloth investor is that I can spend time on the hobbies and leisure pursuits that I enjoy, rather than spending my time tinkering around with my investment portfolio or fretting about the performance of the stock market on a daily basis. You may have taken note of several movie references already during this book. I love going to the cinema and I particularly enjoy the movies of Quentin Tarantino. During the early period of writing this book, I visited the cinema to watch Tarantino's 2019 cinematic release, *Once Upon a Time in... Hollywood*, starring Leonardo DiCaprio, Brad Pitt and Margot Robbie.

Why Many Investors Need a Stunt Double

Pitt's character, a stunt double named Cliff Booth, got me thinking about investors. Undoubtedly, the most notable occasion when investors require a stunt double is during the periodic bouts of volatility that are a natural feature of the stock market. This is because, sadly, too many investors let their emotions get the better of them during these turbulent periods in the market cycle by taking foolish actions, such as selling shares or perhaps even terminating their investing career altogether.

If you're making notes or highlighting sections of this book, then I recommend that you double underline or highlight (or both) the next sentence. Your ability to effectively manage your emotions during periods of market instability will determine your success as an investor.

What is it that causes these customary bouts of volatility

in the stock market? Most of the time, the cause of this volatility in the stock market is *uncertainty*. Generally, there is a positive correlation between company earnings and stock prices, meaning that rising earnings will most likely mean rising stock prices. However, there will be occasions when uncertainty about future earnings growth arises. There are various factors that can potentially affect earnings growth and therefore contribute to this uncertainty.

These factors range from rising unemployment figures, uncertainty about a new political regime in a specific country or perhaps even uncertainty about the severity of an epidemic and the effect it will have on consumer demand (i.e. coronavirus). Quite simply, there are a variety of factors that can cause stock market instability. It is this uncertainty about the future that drives stock prices down.

Uncertainty Is a Certainty!

As human beings, we crave certainty. However, as investors, we must recognise that uncertainty and the resultant volatility that it causes is an inherent feature of the stock market. Unfortunately, our brains are not wired for uncertainty and this is why many people find investing problematic and some choose not to invest at all.

I want you to imagine how many investors there would be if the returns of the stock market always moved in a positive, upwards trajectory with no dips, just one, long, steep diagonal curve from the bottom left to the top right of our fictional, fantasy market graph. Surely everyone would invest then, right? Unfortunately, this fantasy world doesn't exist. The undeniable truth is that volatility functions as the price of entry to the stock market.

Volatility – a Natural Feature of the Investing Landscape

If you are serious about becoming a sloth investor, and you want to be the beneficiary of the outsized returns that have historically been associated with this form of investment, you must recognise that volatility and, further still, bear markets are an essential part of the stock market landscape. Rather than be surprised by these periods of market instability, you must come to expect them, just like a resident of southern France comes to expect 'the mistral' – the strong, cold, north-westerly wind associated with that region of the country.

Or, similarly, if you live in Kansas or Oklahoma in the United States, you should naturally expect the frequent occurrence of tornadoes in your neck of the woods. Likewise, though it may not be easy, as a sloth investor you need to become accustomed to the volatility associated with the stock market.

Accept the Inevitability of Traffic Lights!

I'm somewhat of a Tarantino movie connoisseur and at this stage I can't help but make yet another analogy to one of Tarantino's best-loved movies, *Pulp Fiction*. In a key scene in that movie, Butch (played by Bruce Willis) sits at a traffic light when he locks eyes with Marsellus Wallace, a mob boss that he is seeking to flee from. Incidentally, this scene was inspired by a similar scene in Alfred Hitchcock's 1960 movie, *Psycho*, in which the lead character, Marion Crane, who is making her escape after stealing a significant amount of money from her place of work, notices her boss as he crosses the street as her car is parked at a traffic light. Now, I hear you ask, what has this got to do with investing?

Even Buffett and Bogle Have to Encounter the Red Light

Seeking to invest without suffering volatility is akin to wanting to drive without experiencing red traffic lights. Given their encounters, the respective characters of Butch and Marion wanted to avoid stopping at a red traffic light, but, of course, it is a necessary element – a precondition, if you will – of one's ability to drive. It is important to remember, though, that stopping at a red traffic light is a temporary measure and then you can simply move on.

Likewise, with market volatility, your ability to compound temporarily stops and then it resumes. Even the most successful investors, be they Buffett or Bogle, are unable to avoid the red traffic lights of the investment world. Paradoxically, of course, one could also argue that the red traffic lights of the investment world possess a key benefit in that they enable investors to purchase stocks at a lower price.

Put simply, rather than allowing market volatility to deter you from investing, you must recognise that it's part of the territory of being an investor. Through your investing lifetime, you will experience numerous volatile periods of stock price movement and significant bear markets will affect the value of your portfolio. How you behave during these events will define your success as an investor.

The Good, the Bad and the Ugly

If it's okay with you, I'm going to continue a little more with the cinematic references. Any serious Quentin Tarantino fan knows that his all-time favourite movie is *The Good, the Bad and the Ugly*. Type this film title into a search engine, add Tarantino's name and you'll see interview transcripts in which he comments upon his admiration for this film. You may wonder which path I'm taking you down now. Well, the reason why I'm choosing to reference this film is because I believe that this trifecta of terms – 'the good', 'the bad' and 'the ugly' – provides us with a suitably apt way to describe the mainstream media's perspective of the stock market. As a sloth investor, you must remain headstrong and not allow the mainstream media to cut short your investment journey. A little more now about the good, the bad and the ugly in the field of investment.

There will be times when the behaviour of the stock market is 'good' – when it moves in a characteristically positive way. Interestingly, you will note that during a period such as this, references to the stock market appear less frequently in the mainstream media. Conversely, there will be times when the stock market behaves in a 'bad' way. This is when the stock market swings up and down erratically, causing concern to many investors. The mainstream media's coverage of the stock market is ramped up during these periods. Finally, things get really 'ugly' during bear markets that are characterised by rapid declines and widespread hysterical reportage in the mainstream media. Furthermore, during this 'ugly' period, many investors (wrongly) choose to allow their emotions to override the evidence-led decision-making they should be adhering to.

Although this appears to be an 'ugly' period in the market cycle, to a sloth investor, particularly young sloth investors with a multi-decade time horizon, a bear market is an immense gift. Indeed, the finest gift that the market can bestow upon you while you are patiently building your wealth and investing – i.e. during the accumulating stage of your investing life cycle – is the opportunity to purchase shares on sale.

The Temperamental Toddler

Let me now propose what I consider to be another useful analogy for the stock market. If you're a parent, you may identify with what I'm about to discuss.

I'm a father to two children, a boy and a girl. As a parent, I have had one child go through the 'toddler' stage and, as I write this book, my second child is currently moving through this stage of their existence. Children's behaviour during the toddler stage can be interesting, to say the least. Having witnessed countless toddlers in my role as a parent, I've been able to observe the emotional vulnerability that forms a natural part of a toddler's temperamental terrain.

If we imagine the stock market as an investor, I think it can be useful to characterise it in terms of being a temperamental toddler. Indeed, there are many parallels that can be drawn between the two. It's in a toddler's job description to overreact to things of relatively small significance. Likewise, as an investor, you will learn that the stock market can be subject to extreme mood swings in investor sentiment, particularly in the short term. As you become a more experienced, seasoned investor, you will learn that factors such as job reports, oil price movements and the like have relatively little significance to your portfolio in the long run.

Earlier on in this book, I discussed Benjamin Graham and the reason why I believed he merited inclusion in FIFI – my very own fantasy investing team. You may remember that the key reason why I included Graham is because of his far-sighted formation of 'Mr Market' – an imagined investor, representing the stock market as a whole – whose investment decisions are driven by emotionality instead of sound investment sense.

Benjamin Graham recognised that psychology undoubtedly plays a key role in the success of any investor. The parable of Benjamin Graham's 'Mr Market' teaches us a great deal about how an individual can react to the Shakespearean 'slings and arrows' that define the arena of investing. Unfortunately, many investors allow themselves to fall prey to these 'slings and arrows'.

For example, many individuals fail to understand that periodic bouts of volatility in the stock market is the norm, rather than the exception. As a result, these relatively short-term periods are enough to compel many investors to cut short their investing careers. Of further significance is the fact that these 'slings and arrows' also function to deter many people from investing altogether.

Alternatively, and in a more rational manner, rather than approaching volatility with a furrowed brow, a sloth investor remains calm and instead looks to capitalise from the irrational behaviour of other market participants (non-sloth-like investors). When discussing volatility, it's best to learn from the behaviour of Andrew Hallam. Unfazed by the slings and arrows of varied geopolitical events, Hallam simply stays invested at all times, through good times and bad, demonstrating the mastery of emotions required by a sloth investor.

Cloudy with a Chance of Irrationality?

Moving from the geopolitical to the geographical, one study that I found particularly fascinating to read discovered that cloudy days increased in investors' minds the perceived overvaluation of the stock market.[72] This compelled institutional investors to make more sales on cloudy days when they were in a downright gloomy mood. So, what's the lesson to be learned here? Don't allow weather-based pessimism to cloud your judgement.

Whichever lens you choose to view the stock market through, whether it's a temperamental toddler or Benjamin Graham's 'Mr Market', it's vital to remember that the stock market has an inherent Jekyll and Hyde complexion to it. The stock market can behave in an irrational, unpredictable manner over the short term. Therefore, any attempt to predict the movement of the stock market over such a small time period is futile.

---

72 'Weather-Induced Mood, Institutional Investors, and Stock Returns', by William N. Goetzmann, Dasol Kim, Alok Kumar and Qin Emma Wang (8th September 2014). Published by Social Science Research Network – [ssrn.com/abstract=2323852].

Does a Crystal Ball Really Exist? No, so Ignore Stock Market Forecasts

Switch on the financial news on your television or read the financial media and it won't take long until you're confronted with forecasts of the future movement of the stock market. If you're not careful, a combination of slick media coverage and finance-related jargon could tempt you to begin to take seriously the forecasts that you hear and read about.

Let's think back to the first bedrock principle of a sloth investor: simplicity. So, here's some simple advice: *Ignore* stock market predictions!

Unfortunately, a close friend made the wrong decision based upon such a forecast in late 2016. My friend had recently read a financial news article about the likely negative effects of a Donald Trump presidency on the stock market. Indeed, shortly after reading the article, my friend contacted me to warn me of the perilous effect that Trump's intended geopolitical decision-making could have on our portfolios. Despite my friend's concerns, in true sloth investor fashion, I informed him that he should always remain invested and to ignore the 'clickbait' headlines of the financial media. Unfortunately, my friend did not heed my advice and shortly after Trump acceded to the presidency, he was true to his word, selling a significant percentage of his portfolio.

Was this a good decision? Disappointingly, for my friend, it was not. At the end of 2017, with almost a full calendar year of Trump in office, the American stock market had returned 21.83%.[73] The lesson for my friend? It's best

---

73   Source: [slickcharts.com].

not to try and predict the future; after all, do any of us possess a crystal ball? Instead of behaving like a sloth investor – i.e. doing nothing to his portfolio – my friend attempted to use his fictional crystal ball when the best course of action would have simply been inaction.

Conserve Your Mental Bandwidth!

It's important to remember that the business model of financial news depends on viewer engagement. Increasing viewer engagement brings with it increased income via readership and the selling of advertising space. Despite the evidence in favour of passive investing (instead of an actively managed approach to investing), the financial media continue to promote an 'active' approach to investing for their own economic benefit. Richard Ferri, author of *The Power of Passive Investing – More Wealth With Less Work*, states:

> "Why, then, do financial magazines, newspapers, newsletters, websites, and so on continually suggest that there are ways to select winning active funds? Because it makes money for these companies and the people who provide the advice! Investors will pay for the names of advertised winning funds, even though there's no demonstrated reason why those funds should outperform in the future."[74]

Moreover, viewer engagement with financial media is triggered by appeals to our most basic emotions – i.e. the need to exert some degree of control about the future and, in

---

74   Ferri, R., *The Power of Passive Investing: More Wealth with Less Work* (Gildan Media: 2020).

the case of investing, the desire to obtain knowledge about the future direction of the stock market. Despite this, it will be far better for your mental health if you disregard the soundbite circus of the financial media and its future predictions of the stock market. Instead, conserve your mental bandwidth for other aspects of your life, such as family, friends, your leisure pursuits and your employment.

Fortunately, despite the alarming frequency with which stock market forecasts are commonly made, it is encouraging to note that some financial journalists are beginning to advocate this 'switching off' approach to stock market forecasts. Jeff Sommer of *The New York Times*, a columnist on markets, finance and the economy, writes:

> "Many Wall Street strategists are flagrantly inaccurate. They are about as reliable as a weather forecaster who always calls for balmy sunshine in a city where it rains or snows a lot. It is true that they are right about the market's direction more often than they are wrong. But that's only because most of them say the market will rise in the next year, which happens about 70% of the time." [75]

Cognitive Biases

As humans, being honest with ourselves about our own flaws is incredibly difficult. Commonly, it's far easier to identify other people's flawed thinking than our own. Nevertheless,

75 'Forget Stock Market Forecasts. They're Less Than Worthless' by J Sommer. Published in *The New York Times*, December 2019 – [nytimes.com/2019/12/23/business/retirement/index-fund-investing.html#:%7E:text=In%20fact%2C%20many%20Wall%20Street,often%20than%20they%20are%20wrong].

to be a successful investor requires you to commit to a sufficient degree of self-awareness. This is because your success as an investor will, to a large extent, be determined by the patterns of thinking that you engage in.

Cognitive biases represent ways of perceiving the world that may not reflect reality. As an investor, it is important for you to be aware of how they can function to distort reality. Moreover, recognising their existence can enable you to become wiser, allowing you to learn more about how you think and why you think in particular ways.

There are numerous cognitive biases and a wealth of information available online about them. However, for the sake of brevity, I will now elaborate on six biases that a sloth investor must understand.

Action Bias

Hopefully, you've recognised the importance of ignoring stock market forecasts. Despite this though, you still feel, well, that you should do *something*. It's natural to think this way; it's part of your internal monologue. If we feel unwell, most of us will choose to take medication and if the pain persists, we'll visit a medical professional. Similarly, if our car begins to make a strange noise, we're inclined to investigate ourselves or, if motor car maintenance is not your area of expertise, then it's likely you'll consult a mechanic (if you're fortunate to meet a millionaire mechanic, who's able to teach you about investing, even better). Contrary to this, though, within the field of investing, a sloth investor recognises that inactivity > activity.

Sloth Investors Are Programmed to Do Nothing!

Quite simply, as sentient human beings, we are programmed to *act*, whether this is our own actions or employing others to act on our behalf. What makes the field of investing so unique is that, contrary to so many other aspects of our life, very often the best course of action is to *do nothing*. A key feature of a sloth investor is that he/she adopts a do-nothing approach to investing. It sounds counter-intuitive, doesn't it? Think again about the creature you see on the front cover of the book that you are currently reading. As you know, it's a sloth. Sloths are relatively inactive creatures. Likewise, a sloth investor is inherently motionless (most of the time). I'll leave the final words of this critically important section on action bias to the oracle of Omaha, Warren Buffett. In his 2016 Berkshire Hathaway annual report, Buffett espouses the merits of doing nothing when he states:

> "For investors as a whole, returns decrease
> as motion increases."[76]

Loss Aversion

Are you a sports fan? Do you support a football team, a rugby team or some other sporting team? If you do, then undoubtedly you would have experienced how terrible it feels when your team loses. Doesn't the feeling of loss always seem to hurt more than the amazing feeling you get when your team wins? Naturally, as a fan of Tottenham Hotspur football

---

76   See [berkshirehathaway.com/2016ar/2016ar.pdf].

club, I have experienced the pain of loss on many occasions. It's difficult to forget about those losses. Curiously, it appears far easier to recall the heartbreak than the successes.

Quite simply, loss aversion can be defined as the fear of bad things occurring. Loss aversion has played a key role in the evolution of the human species. According to McDermott, Fowler and Smirnov (2008), the potential for food to become scarce was fatal and so a temperament towards avoiding loss is what caused our ancient ancestors to gather their belongings and hunt and scavenge in a new spot.[77]

Moreover, significant studies have demonstrated that humans care a great deal more about avoiding loss than we do about attaining gain. Writing in the *Scientific American*, Dr Russell Poldrack and his team discovered that:

> "The brain regions that process value and reward may be silenced more when we evaluate a potential loss than they are activated when we assess a similar-sized gain."[78]

The researchers found that the reactions in their subjects' brains were stronger when responding to possible losses than to gains. The researchers labelled this 'neural loss aversion'. Numerous studies have shown that humans regret losses around two and half times more than gains make us feel good.[79]

77 'On the Evolutionary Origin of Prospect Theory Preferences' by Rose McDermott, James H. Fowler and Oleg Smirnov. Published in *The Journal of Politics*, April 2008.

78 'What is Loss Aversion?' by Russell Poldrack. Published by *Scientific American* in July 2016 – [scientificamerican.com/article/what-is-loss-aversion].

79 Kahneman, Daniel, *Thinking, Fast and Slow* (New York: Farrar, Straus and Giroux, 2011).

The connections that we can make between loss aversion and investing are clear. During a sustained period of market volatility or, perhaps even a bear market, a significant number of investors choose to sell their stock positions as the market starts to dip, thereby locking in losses rather than avoiding them altogether by staying the course. In such a scenario, in which loss aversion compels investors to revert to cash, we can plainly see evidence of market timing. This is because these very same investors will likely want to re-enter the market when 'things start to look better'. However, how can these investors know precisely the right time to re-enter? The short answer? They don't. No one possesses a crystal ball. Moreover, while these investors sit on the sidelines, there's a strong possibility that they would have missed out on many of the big gains that occur when the market begins to make its inevitable turn upwards.

For some individuals, the fear of loss looms large and they may choose to never invest at all. While such people may deem this choice as a form of security, this security comes with a significantly high cost. The irony is that although they may deem their actions to be of sound judgement, decisions such as this are unsound, once the effects of inflation are taken into consideration. The decision to allow your cash to stagnate, to not utilise it in the stock market, will inevitably, due to the effects of inflation, lead to an erosion of your purchasing power.

Ingroup Bias

Ingroup bias refers to the tendency for individuals to favourably treat members of their own group compared to other groups. How does this specific bias relate to investing? Let me explain with an example from my own life. As a young man, my view of the stock market was framed by two leading influences: the media and my family. On those occasions when the stock market was mentioned on television or in newspapers, it was invariably because of volatility or a sharp decline. Unfortunately for me, as an eighteen-year-old, I was yet to learn about the media's bias towards negativity.

In addition to this, coming from a family that never invested and that warned me off the (supposed) dangers of investing, my mind was quickly (although wrongly) made up. I was quick to decide that the stock market was definitely not for me. No one in my family had ever invested and so I falsely concluded that it couldn't be the right course of action to take with my money. Little did I know how wrong I was.

A key reason then, which explains my premature, naive decision to never invest, was the influence of my family. Their negative view of the stock market affected my own view, meaning that I allowed ingroup bias to influence my perception of investing. Whether it relates to investing or not, I urge you to consider whether you have ever allowed the groups that you are a part of to act as an echo chamber, thereby potentially causing you to take the wrong course of action. What do you do when you are confronted with a course of action or a perspective that conflicts with your pre-existing views? Do you possess the humility to critique your prior perspective or do you take a mental shortcut and simply refuse to consider whether there may be some validity to an alternative viewpoint or course of action?

In summary, a key reason why it took me so long to even consider investing is that I didn't want to confront the pre-existing views that defined my view of the stock market – i.e. I considered it to be too risky, not for everyday people like me and something best left to the professionals. I had yet to learn the bedrock principles of a sloth investor. I urge you not to make the same mistake as me.

Information Bias – Ignore the 'Triple I' (Irrelevant Investing Information)!

In my discussion of ingroup bias, I briefly referred to how the media influenced my perception of the stock market. A key factor that will determine your success as an investor will be your ability to decide which information should be deemed relevant to you making an informed investment decision. Moreover, ignoring irrelevant information will enable you to form a positive path for yourself. There are innumerable ways that you could allow irrelevant investing information to shape your decision-making process.

You have to remember that much of the investing information that you read online is designed to generate clicks, thereby resulting in additional revenue for the publisher of the content. In addition, the writers of this content are human, like you, and are therefore vulnerable to the same cognitive biases being outlined in this section of the book.

Fear-inducing articles – or, what I call, 'Triple I' articles (irrelevant investing information) – are designed to cause a conflict between your prefrontal cortex and your reptilian brain. When you begin to read articles in the financial media, particularly those that are sensationalist in tone, the temptation is for the impulses of your reptilian brain to take over. However, you must ensure that you allow your prefrontal cortex to quash the impulses of your reptilian brain. So, in conclusion, a sloth investor adds another 'I' to 'Triple I' by simply 'ignoring irrelevant investing information'.

Sunk-cost Fallacy

Have you ever sat through a terrible movie at the cinema simply because you didn't want to throw away the money that you had spent to purchase your seat? If you've ever engaged in behaviour like this, then you've subjected yourself to a cognitive bias known as sunk-cost fallacy. This tendency refers to a pattern of behaviour in which someone continues investing their time/money in a venture simply because they have already committed significant resources towards it, even though, ironically, it may actually be causing that person a loss. Within the realm of investing, a great example would be someone that pays a high fee for an actively managed fund (not a good idea) and they continue to pay the high fees irrespective of that fund's performance. Ultimately, the better alternative would be to radically change course and divert funds to a low-fee index tracker. However, due to the sunk-cost fallacy, some investors opt to persevere with an inferior course of action.

Recency Bias

Recency bias refers to the tendency to extrapolate the recent past indefinitely out into the future. As I write this book, during the time of the coronavirus, there exists a very real prospect that a significant number of people will choose not to invest because of the hysterical financial headlines that accompanied this period in our recent history. To the unseasoned, uninitiated investor, attributing too much weight to the glut of headlines generated during a bear market can result in feelings of despair, with the future looking hopeless. An effective remedy that will help you to reduce the effect of this cognitive bias, is to adhere to a longer-term view of the stock market.

Moreover, instead of bemoaning the recent onset of depressed stock market prices, in converse fashion, a sloth investor, particularly one with a multi-decade time horizon, welcomes the opportunity to purchase stocks at a discount.

A 2018 report initiated by Betterment – the largest, independent online financial advisor in the USA – provides us with a rich illumination of the effects of recency bias on investors. The report, titled 'Betterment Consumer Financial Perspectives Report: 10 Years After the Crash',[80] outlines the results of a survey that was conducted with

---

80   See: [https://www.investopedia.com/insights/how-2008-crisis-changed-how-we-save-and-invest/].

2,000 respondents, eighteen years and older, living in the United States. Of these respondents, 1,602 were at least eighteen years old in 2008 – the time of the market crash. When asked how they felt the US stock market (the S&P 500) had performed since 2008, nearly half the people surveyed (48%) thought that the S&P 500 had not risen in the past ten years and 18% thought it had gone down. The fact that two-thirds of the survey's respondents responded in this way is staggering. During the ten-year period from 2008 to 2018, the return of the S&P 500 was in excess of 300%. So, how can we account for the disparity between people's perceptions of the stock market and the reality? Undoubtedly, the media hysteria surrounding the market crash of 2008, with its bias towards pessimism and alarm, would have been a significant factor.

As a sloth investor, you need to understand the importance of adhering to a long-term investing mindset. Though not easy, you need to question whether you have the tendency to attach too much emphasis on what has recently occurred in the stock market. On the flip side to bear market concerns, if you've been investing during a long bull market, have you come to assume that this will continue forever? If you have, then it's important to prepare yourself for the inevitability of a future bear market. Rather than extrapolating recent market behaviour into the future, it's important to understand the cyclical nature of the stock market and to maintain a long-term investment plan, as this will help you form a natural defence against the danger of recency bias.

Be Humble – Accept Your Foibles

We've now explored six cognitive biases. Understanding each of them will enable you to understand more about the potential pitfalls that may lay ahead of you as an investor – pitfalls that could drastically reduce your ability to grow your hard-earned savings. Daniel Crosby, author of *The Behavioral Investor*, states:

> "The brain and the body, marvels of evolution and design elsewhere, are poorly matched to the specific task of compounding wealth."[81]

So, rather than deny the possibility of you succumbing to the effects of the cognitive biases that have been discussed, it is important to acknowledge the likelihood of your inherent predisposition to some (if not all) of them.

Investor and author James P. O'Shaughnessy states in *What Works On Wall Street*:

> "The key to successful investing is to recognise that we are just as susceptible to crippling behavioural biases as the next person."[82]

---

81 Crosby, Daniel, *The Behavioral Investor* (1st ed.); (Harriman House, 2018).

82 O'Shaughnessy, James P., *What Works on Wall Street, Fourth Edition: The Classic Guide to the Best-Performing Investment Strategies of All Time* (4th ed.); (McGraw-Hill Education, 2011).

Learn from Others:

You can enable yourself to forge a headstrong approach to investing by learning from the accumulated experiences of others during bear market contexts. Shining a spotlight on the decisions taken by others and the consequences of these decisions can strengthen your own resolve to commit to a headstrong, long-term investing mindset.

I will now outline the decision taken by another investor during that most alarming of scenarios: a bear market. Firstly, let me introduce you to J L Collins, author of *The Simple Path to Wealth*. In the book, Collins argues strongly in favour of an indexing approach to investing. However, on his blog, this is what Collins has to say about his reaction to the catastrophic stock market plunge in 1987 known as 'Black Monday', when stocks fell more than 25% (yes, 25% over the course of just one day):

> "It is hard to describe just what this was like. Not even the Great Depression had seen a day like this one. Nor have we since. Truly, it looked like the end of the financial world. As any educated investor does, I knew that the market was volatile. I knew that on its relentless march upwards, there could and would be sharp drops and bear markets. I knew that the best course was to hold firm and not panic. But this. This was a whole 'nother frame of reference. I held tight for three or four months. Stocks continued to drift ever lower. Finally, I lost my nerve and sold. I just wasn't tough enough... Then, of course, and as always, the market began again its relentless climb. The market always goes up. My

> mistake of '87 taught me exactly how to weather all the future storms that came rolling in, including the Class 5 financial hurricane of 2008. It taught me to be tough."[83]

It's both insightful and refreshing to read about Collins' humble reflection on the missteps that he took in 1987. Learning from the mistakes of others, such as those made by J L Collins (notably, how loss aversion compelled him to sell), can help you develop your own headstrong approach to investing. Indeed, as an investor, rather than fear their arrival, you need to actively prepare yourself for the inevitability of cataclysmic events that are similar in scale to 'Black Monday'.

A Tight Grip

At this point, it is worth reflecting on one of the characteristics of sloths. A sloth's claws work opposite to human hands; their default position is a tight grip and they must use force to open them. A tight grip on one's investments is needed by investors, particularly during times of turbulence. A tight grip would certainly have been beneficial to J L Collins during the market crash of 1987. How tight would your grip be?

What action could you take in advance to reduce the potential for your portfolio to plunge so rapidly, whether this is over the course of a week or over the course of one day, like Black Monday?

---

83 'Stocks – Part II: The Market Always Goes Up' by J L Collins. Published on 22nd August 2023 on [jlcollinsnh.com/2012/04/19/ stocks-part-ii-the-market-always-goes-up].

In essence, how could you maintain your grip? One such strategy that you can use is the deployment of bonds. In the next section of the book, entitled 'Considerations for Your Sloth Portfolio', I explain how bonds can be used to de-risk your portfolio.

Sloth Investors Display a Bias Towards Optimism

In episode eighteen of *The Sloth Investor* podcast, entitled 'Smells Like Sloth Spirit', Jason Prohaska (my co-host) and I discuss the importance of optimism to one's success as an investor. We've often referenced our love of movies during the podcast series and we're both fans of Jim Carrey. Indeed, one Jim Carrey movie that can teach investors a key lesson about investing is *Dumb and Dumber*[84] (stick with me).

Dumb and Dumber features Jim Carrey and Jeff Daniels playing two bumbling, immature adults with a lack of common sense and little worldly experience. There's a scene where Lloyd, Jim Carrey's character, an incredibly unsophisticated man, has finally been able to track down a beautiful woman named Mary. He asks her if there is any way that the two of them could end up together as a romantic item. Exhibiting an admirable sense of tact, Mary initially lets him down gently with several evasive answers. Eventually, though, Lloyd insists upon a firm answer about his true chances. Here's the exchange:

Lloyd: What are my chances?
Mary: Not good.

---

84 Farrelly, P, *Dumb and Dumber* (New Line Cinema, 1994).

> Lloyd: You mean, not good, like one out of a hundred?
> Mary: I'd say, more like one out of a million.
> Lloyd: So you're telling me there's a chance!

Isn't this exchange great? Okay, so, at this stage, you could be forgiven for wondering what the connection to investing is. Well, something that struck me when I first watched this scene (and that may have struck you, too) is Lloyd's sense of optimism. Despite the numerical odds being overwhelmingly against him, Lloyd determines that there may be a chance at love after all. Okay, so it may not be much of a chance, but certainly enough of a chance in Lloyd's own mind to be a notable cause for celebration. 'One out of a million' truly are five words that should be enough to crush a man's soul, but not Lloyd. His enduring sense of optimism will enable him to continue to pursue the woman of his dreams (despite the overwhelming numerical odds against him).

Let me be explicit now about the connection to investing. I think we can agree that Lloyd's sense of optimism seems entirely irrational. However, Lloyd remains resolute and positive in the face of seemingly insurmountable numerical odds. My appeal to the readers of this book is to instil your approach to investing with an impenetrable sense of optimism. After all, if we heed the lessons of time, the fourth bedrock principle of a sloth investor, we can see that by remaining optimistic and honouring the principle of time (i.e. patience), the results of investing with a long-term mindset can be truly remarkable. In *The Behavioral Investor*, author Daniel Crosby writes:

> "Probability confirms that optimism ought to be the de-facto position of the well-informed investor."[85]

Through the good times and the bad, the inevitable ups and downs of Mr Market, remaining optimistic is therefore an essential ingredient for investing. Investing your hard-earned income in a low-fee, globally diversified collection of companies for many years is a rational approach to investing that has far better odds of success than one out of a million (sorry, Lloyd!). Therefore, given the odds in your favour, isn't this cause for optimism?

---

85 Crosby, Daniel, *The Behavioral Investor* (1st ed.); (Harriman House, 2018).

Mr Sloth's Summary:

- Looking in the mirror will enable you to discover the biggest obstacle to your success as an investor. Successful investing doesn't require a high IQ, but, rather, high control of one's emotions.
- As human beings, we crave certainty. However, as investors, we must recognise that uncertainty and the resultant volatility that it causes is an inherent feature of the stock market.
- The movement of the stock market on a short-term basis can often appear to make little sense. Erratic and unpredictable, it is comparable to the mood swings of a temperamental toddler.
- Ignore stock market predictions. The business model of financial news depends on viewer engagement. This engagement is triggered by an appeal to your most basic emotions.
- Be humble and honest about your inherent flaws. Developing an understanding of a number of cognitive biases will enable you to become more accepting of your natural abilities as an investor.
- Learn from others. There is great wisdom to be learned from successful investors *and* the mistakes of other investors.

Climb Every Mountain – Reflecting on Mr Sloth's Five Bedrock Principles

During my exploration of the five bedrock principles of a sloth investor, I provided several movie references and their connections to the world of investing. Through no particular choice of my own, a movie that I've seen countless times is *The Sound of Music*. Let me tell you why.

Extended periods of lunchbreak rainfall during my elementary school days would result in my headmistress quirkily assembling students in the school hall to watch *The Sound of Music*.

The Hills Are Alive!

For those unfamiliar with this cinematic work, the opening scene, which introduces the movie's signature tune, 'The Hills Are Alive', features a sumptuous background view of the German alpine mountain range. The scenic background of a mountain range provides me with a suitably apt way to bring my discussion of SLOTH, the five bedrock principles of the sloth investor, to a close. This is because there are tremendous parallels that can be drawn between the field of investing and the field of mountaineering.

The Ups and Downs of the Stock Market

Firstly, successfully scaling a mountain naturally entails plenty of ups and downs. Similarly, the ability to maintain your composure and remain headstrong during the inevitable ups and downs of the stock market will determine your success as an investor.

Tune Out the Noise!

For Maria von Trapp, the lead character of *The Sound of Music*, the hills and mountains of the German alpine region may indeed be alive with the sound of music, but a sloth investor must become accustomed to tuning out the investment noise that they will hear.

For example, on several occasions, I've made reference to the harmful role that the media can exert on our investing mindset. Despite the inevitable temptation to tune into the never-ending forecasts and speculation of the financial media, your job is to simply tune out and *ignore* this investment noise. As Warren Buffett stated in 1998: "Wall Street makes its money on activity. You make your money on inactivity."

A study by Fidelity Investments further underscores this point.[86] Fidelity undertook a study to determine which of their accounts had performed the best. The purpose of the study was to capture information concerning the qualities

---

86 'Fidelity Reviewed Which Investors Did Best and What They Found Was Hilarious' by Myles Udland. Published by *Business Insider* on 4th September 2014 – [businessinsider.com/forgetful-investors-performed-best-2014-9].

of their investors that contributed to the best performance. Fidelity's findings were certainly fascinating. Interestingly, Fidelity discovered that the investor accounts that had been completely forgotten about by their account holders ended up with the best performance. The accounts were not tinkered with or traded in and out of. The account holders simply forgot that they existed.

A Predictable Path?

Mountaineering can be hazardous, to say the least. Taking this into account, a reliable, identifiable path is an absolute necessity. Due to the inherent dangers involved within this leisure pursuit, a degree of predictability is then key.

Likewise, for investors, a good night's sleep is more likely when one can be assured of the reliability of the path or route that has been adopted. Let me explain a little more about this now.

What is something that causes so many investors unnecessary high levels of anxiety? Well, one key thing is decisions. As an investor, you may ask: Did I make the correct decision about the right stock to buy? Did I make the correct decision about the right industry to invest in? Questions such as these keep many investors awake at night.

However, for sloth investors, such questions are simply unnecessary. That's because rather than second-guess which specific stock or which particular sector is going to do well, sloth investors give themself access to the entire stock market by investing in a broadly diversified portfolio.

Such a decision means that sloth investors give themselves exposure to an extremely broad range of stocks across a wide range of sectors.

In addition to saving time and simplifying the investing process, such a decision also leads to something that Jack Bogle referred to as 'relative predictability'.

In the book *The Bogle Effect*,[87] author Eric Balchunas writes about an occasion when he asked Jack Bogle why Vanguard investors seemed so good at not flinching and staying the course during tough market declines. In response, Bogle stated that Vanguard's funds were inherently predictable by nature.

Let's make a comparison between an index fund and an actively managed fund for a moment. An actively managed fund, which is a fund that contains a select group of stocks that have specifically been selected by a small group of professional fund managers may very well underperform.

Simply put, for the individual investor, there's no way of knowing whether an actively managed fund will outperform or not. Indeed, on average, most can't, although a small number do.

However, if you do decide to invest your hard-earned income in an actively managed fund, how can you be sure that you have chosen one of the select few that will outperform?

Crossing your fingers that you have selected one of the few actively managed funds that will outperform isn't exactly a recipe for a good night's sleep.

---

87   Balchunas, Eric., *The Bogle Effect: How John Bogle and Vanguard Turned Wall Street Inside Out and Saved Investors Trillions.* (National Geographic Books: 2022).

On the other hand, investing in a low-fee, broadly diversified index fund provides investors with relative predictability because through all of the ups and downs of the stock market over the past two hundred years, history has shown that the overall stock market always recovered from even the lowest points and moments of true despair.

This is why investing in a low-fee, broadly diversified index fund is sometimes known as a 'Sleep Well At Night' (SWAN) strategy.

A good night's sleep comes from the fact that you don't have to worry about whether you are invested in the right stock or the right sector. As the owner of a broadly diversified index fund, you own the stock market as a whole.

Can I Be Your Sherpa?

I'll now illuminate another similarity between the realm of investing and the leisure pursuit of mountaineering. Climbers wishing to climb Mount Everest often benefit greatly from the experience and skills of sherpas. The word 'sherpa' represents the name of an ethnic group of people who come from the mountains of Nepal. A key function that sherpas perform is to prepare a pathway for foreign climbers to follow.

In writing this book, I hope that I can perform the role of investment sherpa, shining a spotlight on the sloth-like route to investing your money. Moreover, it is my hope that the ordinary people (ordinary people but extraordinary investors) that I mentioned at the start of this book can also perform the role of sherpas.

Finally, I firmly believe that each member of FIFI, my fantasy investing team, can also perform a sherpa-like role for you as you embark on your investing journey. The tracks that they have laid down and the peaks that they have reached in their investing careers, through their accumulated, sage-like experiences, certainly provide plenty for you to learn from.

Considerations for Your Sloth Portfolio

Sloth investors are united by their commitment to the five bedrock principles that have been expanded upon in Chapter 5. However, it's important to note that there is no 'one-size-fits-all' portfolio for each and every sloth investor.

Commonly, the acronym 'IP' is shorthand for 'intellectual property' or 'internet protocol'. However, in this book, I want to use 'IP' to refer to 'investment palate' – i.e. the specific way that a sloth investor chooses to invest. For example, just like each person possesses their own unique taste palate, with specific likes and dislikes pertaining to food, so it is that investors can be defined by their investment palate. Essentially, it is the investor's investment palate, or 'IP', that puts the 'personal' in personal finance.

What's Your Risk Palate?

Despite the bedrock principles forming the foundation for a sloth investor's approach to investing, there are conscious choices that have to be made that will vary among different sloth investors. These decisions will vary depending upon several factors, such as the particular sloth investor's age, risk profile and beliefs concerning certain investments. A sloth investor's investment palette will be determined by such factors.

This section will outline and elaborate key considerations for your very own sloth portfolio.

Introducing Bonds

Living away from your home country for a prolonged period of time can have interesting effects. Growing up in the UK, I possessed no particular affinity for James Bond. If there was an old Bond movie being shown on television and there was nothing better on an alternative channel, then maybe I would watch it, but most likely not.

However, having now lived overseas for over a decade, curiously and quite unexplainably, I've grown more attached to 007, developing an affection for this esteemed British cultural icon. It is reported that the favourite 007 moment of Albert 'Cubby' Broccoli, producer of the James Bond series, is the hair-raising moment in *The Spy Who Loved Me* when the British spy audaciously leaps off a snowy mountainside and then subsequently, stunningly, opens a Union Jack parachute.

Bond is, of course, our classic British hero. Similarly, particularly during times of market volatility, you should also note that bonds can perform a decisive, heroic role for your portfolio. The significance of the use of a parachute is important, as will soon become clear in the parallel to investing that I am about to draw.

The Role of Bonds in Your Portfolio – a Portfolio Parachute

As we've just mentioned Bond in flight, let's deploy an aviation analogy. If we view a globally diversified stock fund (world index/ETF tracker) as our portfolio propeller, pushing and propelling our portfolio ever higher, we can consider the bond component to be our portfolio parachute. This is because, during periods of volatility, bonds are much less volatile than stocks. So, the bond component plays an important role as it slows the rapid descent of your portfolio during those periods of market decline that will, of course, inevitably occur.

Therefore, it's fitting that one of the most iconic Bond movie scenes depicts our hero unravelling a Union Jack parachute, slowing his descent to the ground, because, again, as I think it's an important point worth reiterating, the bond component of your portfolio will function as your portfolio parachute during times of intense market volatility.

Simply put, and if you would excuse the Bond movie pun, the usage of bonds will ensure that there are fewer days when your portfolio scares the living daylights out of you.

What Are Bonds?

A bond is a form of loan that is made to a government or business. Generally, the capital that you invest will be safe as long as the government or business receiving the loan is able to pay the money back with the addition of some interest.

As I detailed before, bonds provide downside protection during sustained periods of market volatility. It's often the case that when stocks go down, the value of bonds will go up. So, yes, while bonds will bring stability to your portfolio, it's important to note that your bond allocation should not be viewed as the component of your portfolio primarily responsible for generating profit. This is the role of the equity (world index tracker) allocation of your portfolio. Simply put, your bond allocation serves to 'de-risk' your portfolio.

Bonds – a Licence to Calm

If James Bond has a licence to kill, the bonds of the investment world have a licence to calm. You should actively consider the stabilising role that they can perform for your portfolio. It is your investment palate or, in other words, your risk profile that will determine the extent to which you decide to utilise bonds.

For example, as an investor in the stock market, and aware of market history, you need to prepare yourself for the fact that there will be occasions (around once a decade) when the market will plunge lower by a percentage of 40 to 50%. If you believe that you are someone that would not be able to stomach such an extreme drop, then you should seriously consider ensuring that there is a significant bond component to your portfolio.

Alternatively, a reliance upon bonds would not be such a priority if you deem yourself to be someone that would be able to 'ride out' such extreme drops mentally, demonstrating the patience necessary to see the market gradually return to its previous levels.

However, theorising about your 'perceived temperament' during severe falls in the stock market and your 'actual behaviour' could be two very different things. Taking a look in the rear-view mirror of market history can enable us to obtain an appreciation for the important role that bonds can play in cushioning the potential decline in investors' portfolios. Let's take a look at three differently constructed portfolios for 2008 (the year of the financial crisis).[88]

2008 Stock Fund – Vanguard Total Stock Market ETF (VTI) Bond Fund – Blackrock US Government Bond (CIGAX)			
Portfolio 1:	Stock allocation 100%	Bond allocation 0%	Return: - 36.98%
Portfolio 2:	Stock allocation 60%	Bond allocation 40%	Return: -20.20
Portfolio 3:	Stock allocation 40%	Bond allocation 60%	Return: -11.81%

Comparing the returns of Portfolio 2 and 3 to Portfolio 1, we can see that the presence of bonds in these portfolios was significant as it ensured a less steep decline in the values of these portfolios.

---

88   Source: [https://www.portfoliovisualizer.com/].

While it should be recognised that bonds perform heroic feats by reducing the severity of market plunges upon your portfolio, it's also important to note that the greater your bond allocation, the less your portfolio will rise when compared to a portfolio with a greater concentration of stocks.

For example, let's take a look at the data for 2013.[89]

2013 Stock Fund – Vanguard Total Stock Market ETF (VTI) Bond Fund – Blackrock US Government Bond (CIGAX)			
Portfolio 1:	Stock allocation 100%	Bond allocation 0%	Return: 33.45%
Portfolio 2:	Stock allocation 60%	Bond allocation 40%	Return: 19.05%
Portfolio 3:	Stock allocation 40%	Bond allocation 60%	Return: 11.85%

What Type of Bond Fund Should You Buy?

As noted earlier, bonds are primarily loans to a government or business. A bond offering by a business is known as a corporate bond. A business will issue a bond in order to raise capital. They are considered to be riskier than government bonds because they are seen to be more likely to default on their debt than stable governments. As a result, corporate bonds will generally offer a higher rate of interest to reflect this added risk.

However, it's important to remember that the role of bonds in your portfolio is to provide *stability*, instead

---

89   Source: [https://www.portfoliovisualizer.com/].

of to drive returns. It's also interesting to note that the performance of corporate bonds often correlates with stocks. Consequently, *government bonds* should be your preferred type of bond as they have a negative correlation to stocks, meaning that when stocks fall, your bonds should remain more stable, thereby helping you to de-risk your portfolio and easing your blood pressure at the same time.

It's important to note that the duration of government bonds varies between short term and long term. I'll now explain the pros and cons of each and why I prefer short-term bonds.

Longer-term bonds tend to pay higher rates of interest compared to short-term bonds. However, longer-term bonds are subject to higher-interest-rate risk. For example, if you purchase a long-term bond that pays 3.5% annually over the next ten years, there's the very real threat that inflation could reduce its purchasing power. This is because the bond may pay 3.5% annually, but if you're buying groceries that increase in price every year by 5%, you're losing to your fruit and vegetables.

Therefore, it is because of these reasons that buying government bond ETFs with shorter-term durations (known as shorter maturities) is usually more sensible than buying longer-term bond ETFs.

When bonds within a government bond ETF mature, they are replaced. If inflation increases, the newly purchased bond will provide interest yields at a higher rate, thereby enabling investors in short-term bonds to not lose out to inflation.

Let's Talk Percentages

The unwritten rule within the field of investing is for an investor to have a bond allocation that is close to their age. So, for instance, a thirty-five-year-old has roughly 35% of their portfolio allocated to bonds and 65% allocated to stocks.

Although this rule of thumb – outlining a rough equivalence between age and bond allocation – is useful, it's important to take account of an individual investor's circumstances. For example, an employee of the government, who is expected to receive a guaranteed pension when they retire, can consequently afford to take on more potential volatility, therefore reducing the allocation of bonds in their investment portfolio.

Also, if all investors were to rigidly adhere to the aforementioned age/bond rule of thumb, wouldn't it therefore naturally follow that a twenty-year-old should have 20% of their portfolio invested in bonds? Again, this is where a degree of nuance is needed. Some would argue that a twenty-year-old, at the beginning of their investing lifetime, should not initially begin with any bond component as they have plenty of time to ride out any market drops in the early stages of their investing career.

Conversely, though, for young investors with even the sternest of stomachs, some would argue that it's important for there to be at least a 10% allocation to bonds. The reason? The rationale that underpins this line of thinking is that an allocation to bonds at the outset of an investing lifetime, even if relatively minimal, develops a good habit – i.e. buying stocks and bonds gets the young investor used to the process of buying both of these elements of a portfolio. Moreover, this bond component helps to formulate and condition, from a young age, the necessary resilience required to be a successful investor.

It's important to remind ourselves that the age/bond ratio is simply a rule of thumb. As such, a degree of flexibility is required by investors to ensure that they don't fall prey to the potential problems that could arise from rigidly adhering to this unwritten rule. For instance, a strict adherence to this rule of thumb would dictate that a seventy-year-old should have 70% of their portfolio in bonds and, therefore, 30% in stocks. For a healthy seventy-year-old, with potentially thirty more years to live, this portfolio allocation could be far too conservative. Yes, bonds are important, but your stock component performs the role of portfolio propellor, thrusting its overall value ever higher.

Should You Deploy Bonds in Your Portfolio?

So, what's my advice? Well, although I may be accused of sitting on the fence, ultimately the decision rests with you. Take a look at yourself. What's your investment palate; what's your risk profile? The use of the term 'palate' is opportune and useful here because of its connection to the theme of food. For instance, do you think that you would be able to stomach the periodic bouts of volatility and, worse still, the roughly once-a-decade jaw-dropping market plunges that are a natural feature of being an investor?

If you're likely to be someone that could panic when confronted with an extreme market plunge, then you should seriously consider allocating a significant amount of your portfolio to bonds. After all, just as James Bond represents the British government's secret weapon, bonds could perform heroic feats for your portfolio when things start to look unsteady. Therefore, the presence of a bond component in your portfolio should certainly be an important consideration. For investors either approaching retirement or having just entered the retirement phase of their life, the mental harm caused by a severe market plunge could be debilitating. This is why bonds should certainly be an important consideration for an investor at this stage in their life.

Rebalancing

The practice of rebalancing the stock and bond components of a portfolio is a routine practice taken by pension funds and numerous individual investors around the world. Rebalancing is linked to the goal allocation of your portfolio.

Your goal allocation is the percentage of your portfolio that is allocated to both stocks and bonds. For example, a forty-year-old may choose to have 40% of their portfolio in bonds and 60% in stocks. Let's say a market crash occurs and this causes the investor's stock allocation to fall to 50%. This means that the forty-year-old now has 50% of their portfolio in stocks and 50% in bonds. The market crash has affected the goal allocation of this investor's portfolio, but the process of rebalancing can enable this forty-year-old to bring their portfolio back to their desired allocation.

How Can You Rebalance?

Following the example from above, the market crash resulted in the forty-year-old investor holding a disproportionate percentage of their portfolio in bonds, which consequently affected their desired stock/bond allocation. To ensure that this investor could return to their desired goal allocation, he/she could sell some of their bond fund to buy more of their stock fund. The sage actions of Andrew Hallam during the financial crash of 2008 can teach us more about how to rebalance. As he explains in a blog post titled, 'Beating the Market with Bonds', Hallam shrewdly capitalised on the availability of plunging stock prices in 2008 to 2009 by selling some of his bond holdings to buy cheaper stocks. He states:

> "I believe (most of the time) in having a high bond allocation matching your age. It ensures that your investments are less volatile as you get older, and it gives the dispassionate investor a fabulous war chest when things get cheap… When the markets fell in 08/09, I started selling off bonds to buy stocks. The lower the markets fell, the more bonds I sold – and the more stocks I bought."[90]

When reflecting on Hallam's decision-making process during this time of rebalancing, a key point to note is that he was able to utilise his bond holdings to buy shares when they

---

90 'Beating the Market with Bonds' by Andrew Hallam. Published on *Andrew Hallam* on 26th May 2010 – [andrewhallam.com/beating-the-market-with-bonds].

were 'on sale' – i.e. after they had experienced a significant drop. So, as we have seen, bonds serve to reduce the volatility of your portfolio, protecting you from extreme drops, but they can also be deployed in a clever, strategic way during a period of steep stock market declines by enabling you to buy stocks at a discount.

When Should I Rebalance?

You can take varied approaches to rebalance your portfolio. As you know, the first bedrock principle of the sloth investor is a belief in simplicity and so here are three simple ways to rebalance:

- On a pre-assigned date once a year: You can decide to rebalance your portfolio on an annual basis by deciding on a set date. For example, this could be your birthday, the first day of the year, your wedding anniversary or any other arbitrary fixed date of your choice.
- Each time you invest new money: When you invest new money, whether this be monthly or quarterly, you can buy the fund(s) that are lagging behind your desired portfolio allocation. For instance, if the bond component is starting to lag, then you will 'prop up' this component of your portfolio by purchasing more of your bond fund. It should be noted that this strategy will generally be fine when your portfolio is relatively small. However, this method will certainly prove more difficult when your portfolio increases to a much larger size.

- When your asset classes diverge from their desired percentage allocation: Instead of seeking to rebalance on a monthly basis, some investors will simply rebalance as and when their allocation has drifted by more than a predefined percentage. So, for example, if your goal allocation has moved by an amount of 5% or more from your target allocation, then it would be time to rebalance.

A core finding from a 2015 Vanguard research brief noted that rather than worrying excessively about *when* to rebalance (e.g. quarterly, annually, etc.), the mere act of rebalancing was itself the key to investor success.[91]

A Rebalancing Example

Suzy is thirty years old and the desired target allocation for her ETF portfolio is: 70% world equity tracker and 30% government bond.

On Suzy's rebalancing day (she chooses her wedding anniversary), she checks her portfolio and identifies that her asset allocation has drifted more than 5% from her desired allocation. In fact, due to a recent market correction, the drift has caused the equity component of her portfolio to fall by 10%, resulting in the following unintended portfolio allocation: 60% world equity tracker and 40% government bond.

---

91 'Best Practices for Portfolio Rebalancing' by Yan Zilbering, Colleen M. Jaconetti and Francis M. Kinniry Jr. Published by Vanguard Research in November 2015 – [financieelonafhankelijkblog.nl/wp-content/uploads/2021/11/Vanguard-ISGPORE.pdf].

Suzy recognises that she needs to rebalance to bring the stock component of her portfolio (the world equity tracker) back up to 70%. On her next monthly portfolio purchase, Suzy could seek to purchase more shares of her world equity fund to bring this component of her portfolio back to its desired goal allocation.

Or in the event that she does not have funds available that month, Suzy could sell some of her government bond shares and buy more shares of her world equity tracker. If she takes this latter option it would look something like this:

Let's assume she has a portfolio of £50,000. The desired allocation would therefore be: £35,000 in her world equity fund (70% of her portfolio) and £15,000 in her bond fund (30% of her portfolio).

However, due to the recent market correction, the fund has drifted, thereby resulting in the following: £30,000 in her world equity fund (60% of her portfolio) and £20,000 in her bond fund (40% of her portfolio).

In order for the desired goal allocation of Suzy's portfolio to get back to where it should be, Suzy recognises that she needs to trim £5,000 from her bond portfolio and reallocate the proceeds of this sale to buy more of her world equity fund.

Let's assume that each share of her bond fund costs £7.75. Suzy then needs to sell roughly 645 of these shares. This is because 645 x £7.75 = £4998,75.

Finally, Suzy will use this amount to buy more shares of her world equity fund. So, let's assume that each share of her world equity fund currently costs £12.80.

Suzy recognises that she can buy 390 shares with the proceeds of her bond fund sale, costing her £4,992 (390 x £12.80).

Rebalancing enables you, the sloth investor, to maintain your desired level of risk exposure, otherwise known as your risk profile. It is a pragmatic process that has long been considered an essential element of long-term investing.

David Swensen, author of *Pioneering Portfolio Management* states:

> "Over long periods of time, portfolios allowed to drift tend to contain ever increasing allocations to risky assets, as higher returns cause riskier positions to crowd out other holdings. The fundamental purpose of rebalancing lies in controlling risk, not enhancing return. Rebalancing trades keeps portfolios at long-term policy targets by reversing deviations resulting from asset class performance differentials. Disciplined rebalancing activity requires a strong stomach and serious staying power".[92]

Rebalancing Sounds Like Too Much Work – Is There a More Sloth-like Option?

Now, after reading about rebalancing, you may well be thinking that you would prefer a more simple, sloth-like strategy. If this is the case, then Vanguard provides options that will take care of rebalancing for you.

---

92 Swensen, David F., *Pioneering Portfolio Management: An Unconventional Approach to Institutional Investment, Fully Revised and Updated* (Updated ed.); (Free Press: 2009).

Vanguard's LifeStrategy funds allocate a fixed amount to equities and a fixed amount to bonds. You can have 20%, 40%, 60%, 80% or 100% in equities. So, for example, the 80% LifeStrategy fund will have 80% in equities and 20% in bonds. Vanguard then ensures that adjustments are periodically made to ensure that the fund's goal allocation is maintained at the same level – i.e. 80% stocks and 20% bonds. I provide more information about Vanguard's LifeStrategy funds in Chapters 7 and 8.

Vanguard UK also provides another option through their Target Retirement funds. These funds initially begin with a fixed ratio of 80% equity and 20% bonds. The investor picks the retirement date that they desire and then you are matched with a corresponding fund. As your retirement date nears ever closer, your fund will increasingly move towards a greater concentration of bonds.

Here is the data for three of Vanguard's Target Retirement funds:

- 2045 fund: 80% equity, 20% bonds
- 2035 fund: 70% equity, 30% bonds
- 2025 fund: 60% equity, 40% bonds

So, although the 2045 fund currently has a high concentration of its fund invested in equities, you can expect to see this heavy equity concentration gradually reduce as that date becomes ever closer. Again, I have provided more information about Vanguard's Target Retirement Funds in Chapters 7 and 8.

Distributing or Accumulating Funds?

One of the decisions that you will need to take when choosing your investment path is whether you prefer to invest in accumulating or distributing funds.

What's the Difference Between Distributing and Accumulating Funds?

A distributing fund periodically distributes dividends to its investors. This usually happens on a quarterly basis, but the dividends can also be distributed on a monthly, biannual and annual basis. The distributing fund is the most common form of investment fund.

An accumulating fund is a relatively new entrant into the realm of investing. Instead of distributing the dividend to the investors of the fund, the accumulating fund reinvests the dividends within the fund. So, despite the fact that the investor maintains the same amount of shares within the accumulating fund, these shares will be worth more.

Is It Better to Invest in Accumulating or Distributing Funds?

Yes, I know that you'll accuse me of sitting on the fence here, but, yet again, the choice comes down to your investment palate and your own individual preference.

Naturally, the most sloth-like form of action would be to invest in an accumulating fund. The reason is that, quite simply, the dividends are taken care of by the investment company and you can happily get on with your life without needing to care about the use of the fund's dividends.

Also, the reinvestment of dividends within an accumulating fund can function to compound your future returns. So, quite simply, if you are seeking to aggressively grow your invested capital, then an accumulating fund will likely be your preferred choice of fund.

Conversely, some investors prefer to invest in a distributing fund because they enjoy receiving the periodic addition of dividend income into their investment account. Moreover, this source of income can then be withdrawn by you to spend on whatever you wish to buy.

You can easily identify whether a fund is distributing or accumulating by looking at the fund's fact sheet online. Finally, it should be noted that you may not necessarily be able to find a distributing or accumulating version for each specific fund that you want to buy.

Mr Sloth's Summary:

- The decisions that you take as an investor should be determined by your 'investing palate'. What's your age? What's your level of risk (your risk profile)? What experience do you have?
- Bonds can potentially play an important role for your investments, functioning as your portfolio parachute during times of intense market volatility.
- Rebalancing enables you to adhere to the 'goal allocation' of your portfolio.
- A distributing fund periodically distributes dividends to its investors. This usually happens on a quarterly basis, but the dividends can also be distributed on a monthly, biannual and annual basis. On the other hand, an accumulating fund reinvests the dividends within the fund.

Vanguard and the Growth of Index Investing

If there were an award for the most appropriate name for a financial organisation, then Vanguard would be a serious contender.

Conduct a simple internet search of the term 'vanguard' and you'll be informed that the word is a noun meaning: 'a group of people leading the way in new developments or ideas'. Moreover, the term 'vanguard' can also mean 'the foremost part of an advancing army or naval force'. Indeed, the company's logo for many years was a grand, majestic-looking ship.

Vanguard, the company, was founded by Jack Bogle and was responsible for launching the first index fund available to all investors in 1976. The fund was called the First Investors Index Trust and it was later renamed the Vanguard 500 Index Fund.

As we approach a half century since the first index fund was made available, one must take a moment to simply stand back in awe at the astonishing impact that Vanguard has had on the investment industry. Robin Wigglesworth, in his book *Trillions*, refers to the growth of Vanguard and the concept of index investing as the 'Manhattan Project of money management'. Full of praise for the immeasurable influence of Bogle, he goes on to state:

> "Vanguard would go on to help millions of people secure more comfortable retirements – and become one of the most disruptive forces in the annals of the investment industry."[93]

Similarly, in his book *The Bogle Effect*, author Eric Balchunas has this to say on the growth of this financial titan:

> "The compounding effect that Vanguard experienced would become a fitting parallel to the compounding effect of buy-and-hold, low-cost index investing that Bogle preached relentlessly for about fifty years. In short: hang in there and don't do anything stupid because it will start to add up."[94]

Blossoming like a flower in spring, the popularity of low-cost, broad-based indexing over the last half century has truly been wondrous to behold.

---

93 Wigglesworth, Robin, *Trillions: How a Band of Wall Street Renegades Invented the Index Fund and Changed Finance Forever* (Penguin, 2021).

94 Balchunas, Eric., *The Bogle Effect: How John Bogle and Vanguard Turned Wall Street Inside Out and Saved Investors Trillions.* (National Geographic Books: 2022).

A Frictionless Experience

The acclaim that has been heaped upon Jack Bogle and Vanguard is fully deserved. For decades, Vanguard really has led the way in providing investors with low-cost, fuss-free, sloth-like investment options. In fact, I would use the term 'frictionless' to describe many of the options that Vanguard has developed for the individual investor. The gravitational pull of this approach to investing can be attributed to its beautiful simplicity and its sheer democratising effect.

This chapter of the book may be considered by some to be one long advertisement for the company. However, for the investor that really does desire a 'minimum fuss, hands-off' approach to investing, Vanguard indeed offers an impressive suite of options.

Let's now dig into the options that Vanguard provides.

Vanguard Funds

There are two broad approaches to investing that you can adopt by using Vanguard. I refer to these as 'Off the Shelf' and 'Do It Yourself' (DIY).

A key decision that you will need to consider before using Vanguard is recognising which of these two approaches ('Off the Shelf' or 'DIY') is best for you. Therefore, knowing oneself – i.e. knowing one's investing palate – is important here. If you really do want to remain utterly sloth-like in your approach to investing, then the ready-made, 'Off-the-Shelf' approach that I outline below will probably be best for you.

On the other hand, if you're keen to be a little less sloth-like and want to build your own portfolio, then the 'Do-It-

Yourself' approach that I outline below will probably be the best fit for you.

Off the Shelf

Vanguard provides investors with two core, ready-made investment options. These are:
1. LifeStrategy funds
2. Target Retirement funds

- Vanguard's LifeStrategy Funds

Vanguard's ready-made LifeStrategy funds enable you to invest globally while minimising the inconvenience of managing your own investment portfolio.

What Are the LifeStrategy Funds?

A LifeStrategy fund consists of multiple individual index funds in one portfolio fund. You'll sometimes hear such a fund referred to as a 'fund of funds'. This is because a LifeStrategy fund provides you with access to thousands of equity (stocks) shares and bonds in a single investment.

The Benefits of a LifeStrategy Fund

The 'blended' characteristics of the LifeStrategy funds enable you to reduce risk by spreading your investments across both stocks and bonds. The reduction in risk stems from the inherent characteristics of both asset classes.

Yes, historically, stocks have provided investors with greater returns over the long run, but they are the riskier asset class to own. Conversely, bonds, as I have previously outlined earlier in the book, offer more stability at the expense of lower potential returns.

It is this blended approach that makes the LifeStrategy funds appealing, for they provide investors with the opportunity to extract 'the best of both worlds'.

The LifeStrategy funds provide a truly off-the-shelf, frictionless way to invest as no rebalancing is required and everything is done for you.

Finding the Right LifeStrategy Fund for You

If what you have read about the LifeStrategy funds so far seems appealing, the next step is to align your investment palate with the most appropriate LifeStrategy fund.

In this respect, two of the key factors to address are:
1. Your risk profile
2. Your time horizon

• Your Risk Profile
If you consider yourself to be a particularly cautious investor, then it's likely that you'll want to select a LifeStrategy fund with a greater % weighting to bonds than shares. Conversely, if you're willing to accept a more volatile ride, then it's likely that you'll want to select a LifeStrategy fund that has a greater % exposure to stocks than bonds.

• Your Time Horizon
A central factor for any investor is the amount of time that you are able to invest for. Quite simply, the longer you invest,

the more time you will be able to navigate and overcome the inevitable ups and downs of the market. Therefore, if you have a significant amount of time on your side, it's likely that a LifeStrategy fund with more shares and fewer bonds could be a better fit for you.

The LifeStrategy Funds

Okay, it's about time that we take a look under the hood of the Vanguard LifeStrategy funds to see what is available to you.

Typically, Vanguard offers five LifeStrategy funds. As outlined before, each fund can be distinguished by the unique blend of stocks and bonds contained within them. Here are the funds:

- LifeStrategy 20% equity fund. Shares 20% Bonds 80%
- LifeStrategy 40% equity fund. Shares 40% Bonds 60%
- LifeStrategy 60% equity fund. Shares 60% Bonds 40%
- LifeStrategy 80% equity fund. Shares 80% Bonds 20%
- LifeStrategy 100% equity fund. Shares 100% Bonds 0%

The first fund listed above, the LifeStrategy 20% equity fund, is presented by Vanguard as 'lower risk' and 'lower reward' and for those with shorter-term goals (three to five years) – i.e. perhaps someone close to retirement. The lower risk stems from the fact that the fund has only a 20% exposure to equities (stocks).

On the other hand, the LifeStrategy 60% fund with a 60% allocation to stocks and a 40% allocation to bonds is considered by Vanguard to be appropriate for individuals with medium to longer-term goals (5+ years).

As you would expect with Vanguard, the fees for the LifeStrategy range are low, typically around 0.15% – 0.20%, depending on your location.

Does the 'Off-the-Shelf' complexion of the LifeStrategy funds appeal to you? If the answer is yes, then it will be in your best interest to turn introspective and critically consider your risk profile. How likely are you going to be able to handle the periodic bouts of volatility that intermittently affect the stock market? Would you be able to stomach such occasions? Remember, knowing oneself is critical to being a successful investor.

• Vanguard's Target Retirement Funds

Vanguard's Target Retirement funds represent the second off-the-shelf investment opinion provided by this fund management company. So, what is a Target Retirement fund?

A Target Retirement fund makes investing for retirement very simple. Remember, the first bedrock principle of a sloth investor is *simplicity*!

The simplicity of a Target Retirement fund lies in the fact that you simply select a fund based on when you plan to retire and Vanguard then steers your investment portfolio accordingly. On your behalf, Vanguard will ensure that your Target Retirement fund (should you opt to invest in one) is rebalanced automatically.

That's right, as you begin to age and the grey hairs start to emerge, and the wrinkles become ever deeper, Vanguard will gradually change the asset allocation of your chosen Target Retirement fund.

So, how exactly does that work? Well, as you become older and move closer to retirement, Vanguard alters the composition of your Target Retirement fund by ensuring that it becomes increasingly constructed by lower-risk, more stable investments – i.e. bonds.

Vanguard's Target Retirement funds are named by year – i.e. the year in which you plan to retire. Don't worry about the year in the fund's name. Unlike a container of milk, a Target Retirement fund doesn't have an expiration date. It's simply a name and certainly not to be thought of as some sort of 'Best Before' warning. For instance, in 2031, investors will still be able to purchase a Vanguard Target Retirement 2030 fund.

Let's now take a look at some examples of how Target Retirement funds work, which will help to make things clear.

• Keira

Let's begin with Keira. Keira plans to retire in 2063, which is around forty years away (from the publication of this book). Therefore, either the Target Retirement fund 2060 or the Target Retirement fund 2065 will be appropriate sloth-like investment vehicles for Keira's investment needs.

The significant period of time before Keira's retirement date is reflected in the composition of both of the aforementioned Target Retirement funds. Indeed, they both have the same exact composition (at the current date of writing), which is 90% stocks, 10% bonds. Again, to be clear, why is there such a high % of this fund allocated to stocks? Well, despite the fact that stocks are a riskier asset class than bonds, they offer bigger potential returns.

Moreover, as Keira will have time on her side, she will be able to navigate the inevitable ups and downs that characterise investments in the stock market. It's important to remember though that as Keira moves ever closer to retirement, her fund's allocation will change, as Vanguard will work to reduce the weighting of the fund in stocks, consequently resulting in an increased allocation to bonds.

• Leo

Leo is planning to retire in 2031, which is roughly thirty years before Keira intends to retire. Therefore, Vanguard's Target Retirement fund 2030 will most likely be the best option for him. What difference does this earlier retirement date make? You've guessed it: Leo's retirement fund has a greater percentage allocation to bonds. At the current date of writing (2023), the Target Retirement fund 2030 has around a 65% allocation to stocks and a 35% allocation to bonds.

Again, it's important to be clear about why Leo's Target Retirement 2030 fund has around a 25% greater allocation to bonds than Keira's fund. As Leo is relatively close to retirement, a goal that should be foremost in his mind should be the *preservation* of his investment capital as opposed to seeking to make larger and larger potential gains with stocks. How can Leo work towards achieving this goal? By deploying his capital in a Target Retirement fund that has a significant weighting towards bonds.

Remember, as he is so much closer to retirement than Keira, he has less time to ride out a market crash than she does. Therefore, the more appropriate Target Retirement fund for Leo is one that doesn't tilt as heavily in favour of stocks, the riskier asset class. After all, who wants to be so negatively affected by a stock market slump just before reaching retirement?

The DIY Approach to Using Vanguard Funds

If you're someone that would like to take a more DIY approach to investing, then you could build a simple two-fund portfolio using Vanguard funds.

For instance, with a little more effort than the aforementioned 'Off-the-Shelf' options, you could construct your own DIY approach to investing like a sloth by regularly purchasing a low-fee, globally diversified ETF (in combination with a bond fund, should your investing palate so desire). In Chapter 8, I will provide some examples of how this could be done.

Okay, before you dive into Chapter 8 to learn about the specific Vanguard funds that are open to you, I'll now take some time to linger on some additional questions.

What About Other Fund Providers?

It's undeniable that there has been an explosion in the growth of index investing in recent years.

Therefore, at this point, some readers may naturally be wondering why I haven't provided information on other providers such as Schwab, iShares and other low-cost providers.

The primary reason for this stems back to the first bedrock principle of the sloth investor: *simplicity*! Yes, I certainly could have provided product offerings by these other low-cost providers. However, a key reason why I didn't is for the sake of simplicity.

It's important to remember that whether it's a low-fee, globally diversified fund offered by Vanguard, Schwab, iShares or some other low-cost provider, the composition of these funds will be very similar. As Andrew Hallam states in *Millionaire Expat – How to Build Wealth Living Overseas*:

> "This is a bit like asking 'Should I buy my bananas from Walmart or Safeway?' If two ETFs track the same market, you're buying the same bananas… It matters little, for example, whether you choose Vanguard, iShares, or Schwab. These are three of the biggest names in the world of ETFs. As such, they're good at tracking stock market returns and their costs are competitive."[95]

So, dear reader, my decision to simplify the product offering that I have exposed you to within the next chapter arises from my firm belief in the profoundly important notion of 'keeping it simple' and reducing the number of pages that my beloved readers have to plough through. Moreover, the potential for the hazardous mental mind trap of 'analysis paralysis' was a further consideration that influenced my decision not to provide an exhaustive range of product offerings by other low-cost providers.

---

95   Hallam, Andrew. *Millionaire Expat: How to Build Wealth Living Overseas* (2nd ed.), (Wiley: 2018).

When confronted with too much data, human beings can sometimes be inclined to become paralysed, resulting in no course of action or solution being taken. Barry Schwartz, an American psychologist, writes about this in his book *The Paradox of Choice*.[96] Interestingly (particularly given the title of this chapter), in the book he makes reference to a Vanguard retirement plan study. The study found that employee participation in retirement plans was higher when employers provided them with fewer investment choices. When confronted with too many options, people tended to hesitate, becoming unsure of which option to select and, ultimately, many didn't invest.

This explains why in Chapter 8 I generally (with one or two exceptions) only provide information on Vanguard's funds. I am seeking to do whatever I can to get your investment journey started, instead of becoming stuck in a state of paralysis.

Taking the above into account, though, should you wish to learn more about the product offerings of companies such as Schwab, iShares or some other low-cost provider, I encourage you to conduct some simple online searches. As you would expect, there is now a wealth of information online concerning index funds and it shouldn't take you long to retrieve the information that you desire.

---

96 Schwartz, Barry, *The Paradox of Choice: Why More Is Less* (Harper Perennial: 2005).

Sample Portfolios for a Sloth Investor

What Type of Sloth Investor Are You?

I hope that you found it illuminating to learn more about the two 'Off-the-Shelf' investing options that I expanded upon within the previous chapter.

Perhaps you're someone who considers themself to be an 'Ultra Sloth Investor' – i.e. someone that really wants to make investment as simple as possible. If this is indeed the case for you, then it's likely that you'll opt for one of Vanguard's LifeStrategy funds or, instead, you may opt for one of their Target Retirement funds. After all, both of these funds take care of the rebalancing for you.

As has been previously noted, Vanguard's LifeStrategy funds free you from the hassle of rebalancing, ensuring a consistent allocation to your preferred combination of stocks and bonds. Similarly, Vanguard's Target Retirement funds automatically rebalance over time, as an investor moves ever closer to retirement.

On the other hand, if you wish to take the time to build your own 'Do-It-Yourself' (DIY) sloth portfolio, then choosing a simple two-fund portfolio combination of a low-fee globally diversified portfolio in combination with a bond fund will be an option for you. Remember, though, unlike Vanguard's LifeStrategy and Target Retirement funds, it's going to be up to you to rebalance this DIY portfolio.

Let's now run through a quick example to examine how building a two-fund, DIY portfolio would work. For instance, let's say, as a DIY sloth investor, you want to consistently maintain a roughly 75% exposure to stocks and an accompanying 25% exposure to bonds. However, let's say that in one year stocks perform incredibly well, nudging your exposure to stocks to 85% and thereby reducing your bond exposure to 15%.

So, if you're committed to maintaining a consistent allocation of 75% exposure to stocks and an accompanying 25% exposure to bonds, then you will consequently need to rebalance your portfolio by selling some of your global stock market index to ensure that you get back to your original desired allocation (moving from an 85% to 75% exposure). With the proceeds of this selling of your global stock market index, you would then need to purchase shares of your bond market index, ensuring that you are able to get back to your original desired allocation of 25%.

Alternatively, instead of selling some of your global stock market index to get back to your desired stock/bond allocation, you could simply make sure that your next payment inflows are targeted towards the bond component of your portfolio.

If the above sounds like too much effort, then it's probably best that you adopt 'ultra-sloth' mode and invest in an investment vehicle such as a LifeStrategy or Target Retirement fund.

Within this section of the book, I provide both 'Off-the-Shelf' and 'Do-It-Yourself' (DIY) options for investors from around the globe.

Your Risk Profile (Investment Palate)

The portfolio that you ultimately select should be influenced by your risk profile, or, what I referred to in Chapter 6 as your 'investment palate'. Consequently, here are some questions for you to consider:

- Loss sensitivity – Although admittedly difficult to predict, how would you react if your portfolio were to plummet by 25%? If it's likely that such an incidence would cause you mental distortions, then I suggest a significant allocation to bonds. After all, as I've previously detailed in this book, bonds perform a parachute-like role for your portfolio during significant stock market declines, ensuring a far less damaging descent for your portfolio.
- Experience – What is your experience of investing? Naturally, you may expect that a young investor, in their late teens or early twenties, would opt for a portfolio that is 100% stocks. After all, such an individual is generally going to be multiple decades away from retirement. However, one also has to take into account

the behavioural aspect of investing. For instance, let's say a relatively young investor has chosen to go down the route of selecting a portfolio that is defined by a 100% allocation to stocks. Now, let's hypothesise that within months of beginning their investing journey, this investor's portfolio is then subject to a plunging decline in their portfolio, perhaps due to an unexpected geopolitical event or a problem that has occurred in the money markets. This sudden decline then has the unfortunate effect of giving this novice investor 'the spooks' and they choose never to invest again. We can now see how, at a young age, even a modest allocation to bonds could have a beneficial impact on investor behaviour, by shielding an investor from their worst enemy (themself!).

For the sake of clarity, let me try to be as clear here as I can: I am not saying that each and every investor, of whatever age, should have an allocation to bonds. However, one cannot deny the ability of bonds to soften the blow of the drastic downturns that occasionally characterise the stock market as a whole.

Conversely, if, after a long, hard look in the mirror, you genuinely believe that you have the stomach to withstand the intermittent declines that are an inherent feature of the stock market, then a high percentage allocation to stocks in your portfolio will be what fits you best.

As Socrates stated, 'Know thyself!'

American Sloth Investors

Sample Sloth Portfolios

Sloth investors based in America can purchase 'Off-the-Shelf' portfolios through providers such as Vanguard, Fidelity and Schwab. For the sake of simplicity, though (remember my first bedrock principle?), I'm using Vanguard here.

American sloth investors can buy any of the 'Off-the-Shelf' funds outlined below directly from Vanguard.

LifeStrategy Funds

Name of Fund	Ticker Symbol	Stocks %	Bonds %
Vanguard LifeStrategy Growth Fund	VASGX	80%	20%
Vanguard LifeStrategy Moderate Growth Fund	VSMGX	60%	40%
Vanguard LifeStrategy Conservative Growth Fund	VSCGX	40%	60%
Vanguard LifeStrategy Income Fund	VASIX	20%	80%

Target Retirement Funds

Name of Fund	Ticker Symbol	Stocks %	Bonds %
Vanguard Target Retirement 2025	VTTVX	55%	45%
Vanguard Target Retirement 2030	VTHRX	65%	35%
Vanguard Target Retirement 2035	VTTHX	75%	25%
Vanguard Target Retirement 2040	VFORX	80%	20%
Vanguard Target Retirement 2045	VTIVX	85%	15%
Vanguard Target Retirement 2050	VFIFX	90%	10%
Vanguard Target Retirement 2055	VFFVX	90%	10%
Vanguard Target Retirement 2060	VTTSX	90%	10%

Do It Yourself

Are you an American sloth investor looking to build your own portfolio? Well, you can do so by regularly purchasing the two funds in the table below. Remember, though, unlike Vanguard's LifeStrategy and Target Retirement Funds, it's going to be up to you to rebalance this DIY portfolio.

Vanguard's Total World Stock ETF (VT) provides exposure to a staggering 9,536 stocks. Want to own the world? Well, the VT fund enables you to do so.

The fund contains stocks from every corner of the globe, including both developed and emerging markets. The fund provides American sloth investors with a strong, solid exposure to North American equities (at around 63%).

Vanguard's Total Bond Market Index Fund holds US Treasury, agency bonds, home mortgage securities, high-quality corporate bonds and a small number of foreign bonds.

Ticker Symbol	Name of Fund	What Is It Invested In?
VT	Vanguard Total World Stock ETF	Global Stocks
BND	Vanguard Total Bond Market Index Fund ETF	Holds US Treasury, agency bonds, home mortgage securities, high-quality corporate bonds and a small number of foreign bonds

British Sloth Investors

Sample Sloth Portfolios

British sloth investors can buy all of the 'Off-the-Shelf' funds below directly from Vanguard UK. Automatic deposits can be created, thereby enabling Brits to make regular payments from their bank account into the LifeStrategy fund of choice or, alternatively, into one of Vanguard's UK Target Retirement funds.

These funds will provide British sloth investors with exposure to British shares, North American shares, shares of other developed stock markets and shares of emerging markets. With the exception of the LifeStrategy 100% equity fund, they also include exposure to bonds.

The funds are rebalanced on a regular basis, thereby ensuring the fund's target allocation between stocks and bonds is consistently maintained.

LifeStrategy Funds

Name of Fund	Ticker Symbol	Stocks %	Bonds %
Vanguard LifeStrategy 100% Equity	GB00B41XG308	100%	0%

Vanguard LifeStrategy 80% Equity	GB00B4PQW151	80%	20%
Vanguard LifeStrategy 60% Equity	GB00B3TYHH97	60%	40%
Vanguard LifeStrategy 40% Equity	GB00B3ZHN960	40%	60%
Vanguard LifeStrategy 20% Equity	GB00B4NXY349	20%	80%

Target Retirement Funds

Name of Fund	Ticker Symbol	Stocks %	Bonds %
Vanguard Target Retirement 2025	VTTVX	55%	45%
Vanguard Target Retirement 2030	VTHRX	65%	35%
Vanguard Target Retirement 2035	VTTHX	75%	25%
Vanguard Target Retirement 2040	VFORX	80%	20%
Vanguard Target Retirement 2045	VTIVX	85%	15%
Vanguard Target Retirement 2050	VFIFX	90%	10%
Vanguard Target Retirement 2055	VFFVX	90%	10%
Vanguard Target Retirement 2060	VTTSX	90%	10%

Do-It-Yourself Two-Fund Portfolio

Are you a British sloth investor looking to build your own portfolio? Well, you can do so by regularly purchasing the two funds in the table below. Remember, though, unlike Vanguard's LifeStrategy and Target Retirement funds, it's going to be up to you to rebalance this DIY portfolio.

The global stock component, Vanguard's FTSE All World UCITS ETF, provides investors with exposure to almost 4,000 stocks in nearly fifty countries, which includes both developed and emerging markets. Want to own the world? Well, the VWRL fund definitely ticks the box!

The second component of this DIY portfolio, Vanguard's UK Gilt UCITS ETF, provides exposure to UK government bonds.

Ticker Symbol	Name of Fund	What Is It Invested In?
VWRL	FTSE All World UCITS ETF	Global Stocks
VGOV	UK Gilt UCITS ETF	UK Government Bonds

Canadian Sloth Investors

Sample Sloth Portfolios

Canadians can purchase any of the ETFs listed in the table below from any of Canada's brokerages. These funds will provide Canadian sloth investors with exposure to Canadian shares, US shares, shares of other developed stock markets and shares of emerging markets. They all provide exposure to bonds except for the iShares Core Equity ETF Portfolio (XEQT).

Ticker Symbol	Name of Fund	Stocks %	Bonds %
XEQT	iShares Core Equity ETF Portfolio	100%	0%
XGRO	iShares Core Growth ETF Portfolio	80%	20%
XBAL	iShares Core Balanced ETF Portfolio	60%	40%
XCNS	iShares Core Conservative Balanced ETF Portfolio	40%	60%
XINC	iShares Core Income Balanced ETF Portfolio	20%	80%

Do-It-Yourself Three-Fund Portfolio

Are you a Canadian sloth investor looking to build your own portfolio? Well, if you're eagle-eyed, you would have noticed the slight change from a two-fund portfolio to a three-fund portfolio in the heading above.

What's the reason for this? Quite simply, it's because the Vanguard FTSE Global All Cap (VXC) excludes an exposure to Canada. Therefore, to ensure exposure to their domestic stock market, Canadian sloth investors would need to purchase an additional fund, which is the Vanguard FTSE All Cap ETF (VCN).

Canadians must remember, though, that the Canadian stock market only accounts for around 3% of global stock market capitalisation. So, if you're a Canadian sloth investor, it's important to ensure that you don't succumb to home bias towards your country's domestic stock market.

This three-fund DIY portfolio for Canadians is rounded out by the Vanguard Canadian Short-Term Bond Index ETF (VSB).

Ticker Symbol	Name of Fund	What Is It invested In?
VXC	Vanguard FTSE Global All Cap ex Canada ETF	Global Stocks (excluding Canada)
VCN	Vanguard FTSE Canada All Cap ETF	Canadian Stocks
VSB	Vanguard Canadian Short-Term Bond Index ETF	Canadian Bonds

Australian Sloth Investors

Sample Sloth Portfolios

Each of the 'Off-the-Shelf' funds below provide Australian investors with exposure to Australian shares, North American shares, shares of other developed stock markets and shares of emerging markets. Lastly, these funds provide exposure to both Australian bonds and global bonds. These funds are rebalanced on a regular basis, thereby ensuring that the fund's target allocation between stocks and bonds is consistently maintained.

Ticker Symbol	Name of Fund	Stocks %	Bonds %
VDHG	Vanguard Diversified High Growth Index	90%	10%
VDGR	Vanguard Diversified Growth Index	70%	30%
VDBA	Vanguard Diversified Balanced Index	50%	50%
VDCO	Vanguard Diversified Conservative Index	30%	70%

Do-It-Yourself Three-Fund Portfolio

Are you an Australian sloth investor looking to build your own portfolio? Well, if you're eagle-eyed, you would have noticed the slight change from a two-fund portfolio to a three-fund portfolio in the heading above.

What's the reason for this? Quite simply, it's because the Vanguard International Shares Index Fund (VGS) does not contain exposure to Australian shares. Therefore, to ensure exposure to their domestic stock market, Australian sloth investors would need to purchase an additional fund, which is the Vanguard Australian Shares Index Fund (VAS).

Aussies must remember, though, that the Australian stock market only accounts for around 2% of global stock market capitalisation. Most of the Australians that I have known have been a patriotic bunch. However, if you're an Australian sloth investor, it's important that you ensure that this patriotism doesn't result in a home bias towards your country's domestic stock market.

This three-fund DIY portfolio for Australians is rounded out by the Vanguard Australian Fixed Interest Index Fund (VAF), an Australian bond index.

Ticker Symbol	Name of Fund	What Is It Invested In?
VGS	Vanguard International Shares Index Fund	The Global Stock Market
VAS	Vanguard Australian Shares Index Fund	The Australian Stock Market
VAF	Vanguard Australian Fixed Interest Index Fund	Australian Bonds

European Sloth Investors

Sample Sloth Portfolios

In Europe, only residents of the UK are currently able to open an account with Vanguard. Therefore, this means that in terms of the convenience of buying Vanguard's products, if you are a resident of any other European country, you are at a slight disadvantage to British sloth investors.

However, does this mean that if you're based in Europe that you can't invest like a sloth? Absolutely not! This is because you can still invest in Vanguard ETFs through different investment platforms such as Interactive Brokers, eToro and DEGIRO. Let's take a look first, though, at Vanguard's LifeStrategy range, which is available to European sloth investors.

These 'Off-the-Shelf', all-in-one portfolios could be bought on either the German or Italian stock exchanges. Each of the funds below are priced in Euros. These funds are globally diversified with a roughly 60% exposure to American stocks in their equity component.

Name of Fund	Ticker Symbol on Xetra[97]	Stocks %	Bonds %
Vanguard LifeStrategy 80% Equity	V80A	80%	20%
Vanguard LifeStrategy 60% Equity	V60A	60%	40%
Vanguard LifeStrategy 40% Equity	V40A	40%	60%
Vanguard LifeStrategy 20% Equity	V20A	20%	80%

Do It Yourself

Are you a European sloth investor looking to build your own portfolio? Well, you can do so by regularly purchasing the two funds in the table below. Remember, though, unlike Vanguard's LifeStrategy funds, it's going to be up to you to rebalance this DIY portfolio.

As I outlined in the beginning of this section, despite not having access to the Vanguard platform (unlike British sloth investors), other Europeans can still invest in Vanguard ETFs through different investment platforms such as Interactive Brokers, eToro and DEGIRO.

A simple two-fund portfolio for European sloth investors is easy to achieve. Firstly, let's take a look at the stock component.

Vanguard's FTSE All World UCITS ETF (VWCE) undoubtedly ticks the box of providing global diversification,

---

97   This is the ticker symbol for these funds on the German stock exchange, based in Frankfurt.

enabling European sloth investors to gain exposure to almost 4,000 stocks in nearly fifty countries, which includes both developed and emerging markets.

The second component of this DIY portfolio, Vanguard's Eurozone Government Bond UCITS ETF (VETY) provides exposure to a broad spread of Euro denominated bonds.

Ticker Symbol	Name of Fund	What Is It Invested In?
VWCE	FTSE All World UCITS ETF	Global Stocks
VETY	Eurozone Government Bond UCITS ETF	Eurozone Government Bonds

Other Nationalities

Sample Sloth Portfolios

Okay, so the mission of the author of this book is to 'simplify investing for all'. This means that Mr Sloth does not want to exclude any nationality from the opportunity of accessing the greatest wealth machine known to mankind: the stock market!

So far, I have provided information for much of the world. However, should you find that your country has not been represented, my suggestion is to build a simple two-fund portfolio that is available from one of the most accessible stock exchanges in the world: the London Stock Exchange.

No specific laws prohibit non-UK citizens from investing in the UK stock market. Therefore, investors outside of the United Kingdom can usually access this stock exchange, providing them with the opportunity to build their own portfolio of low-cost investment funds.

Below, you will find a sample portfolio for international sloth investors.

The global stock component, Vanguard's FTSE All World UCITS ETF, provides investors with exposure to almost 4,000 stocks in nearly fifty countries, which includes both developed and emerging markets. Want to own the world? Well, the VWRL fund definitely ticks the box!

The second component of this DIY portfolio, the iShares Core Global Aggregate Bond UCITS ETF, provides exposure to global government bonds.

Ticker Symbol	Name of Fund	What Is It Invested In?
VWRL	FTSE All World UCITS ETF	Global Stocks
AGGG	iShares Core Global Aggregate Bond UCITS ETF	Global Government Bonds

Sloth Investors in Action
(Or Should That Be Inaction?)

I hope by now that you have been able to recognise and appreciate the overwhelming evidence in favour of 'investing like a sloth' – i.e. choosing to invest in a simple, low-fee and diversified manner in an inactive way.

Whether it's Warren Buffett's advocacy for index funds, the preference of Michael Lewis (author of books such as *Moneyball* and *The Big Short*) for this style of investing or perhaps even the success story of Andrew Hallam, aka the 'Millionaire Teacher', my hope is that you have been able to form a clear picture of the benefits of this approach to investing.

However, let's put Warren, Michael and Andrew to the side for now and hear from some individuals based around the world that have been kind enough to share with Mr Sloth their approach to investing. So, what follows are several examples of 'real-life' actual sloth investors. The rationale for their inclusion within this book is so that you can see how other people approach their investment decision-making.

Example 1:
Name: Jess Gosling
Age: 45
Location: Taiwan

Why do you invest?
I invest as I have no retirement plan, except this! It made sense to me as receiving less than 0.5% interest in my bank accounts would never support retirement. I also invest to raise a bulk sum for my daughter when she hits eighteen for university or a car/house, whichever she chooses.

What advice would you give to someone just getting started on their investment journey?
Read up all that you can. I recommend Andrew Hallam's book, *Millionaire Expat*, as it's pretty clear and digestible. I also contacted Mark Zoril, as recommended by Andrew Hallam, to set up my brokerage account.

How do you invest?
I invest on the London Stock Exchange. I invest approximately 70% in global stock ETFs and 30% in bond ETFs. They are both with Vanguard.

Example 2:
Name: Tom Bannister
Age: 41
Location: Thailand

Why do you invest?
I'm saving for the future. I am keen to build a portfolio to fund both my retirement and my children's future.

What advice would you give to someone just getting started on their investment journey?
Start as soon as possible. Also, read Andrew Hallam's books and ensure you invest consistently every month – use dollar-cost averaging rather than trying to 'play the game' in the investment world. Time in the market is better than timing the market.

How do you invest?
I purchase ETFs every month on Swissquote.

Which resources (books, online sites, social media feeds, etc.) have you found useful in terms of your investment education?
Andrew Hallam's book – *Millionaire Expat*.

Example 3:
Name: Callum Thurley
Age: 32
Location: Dubai, United Arab Emirates

Why do you invest?
I invest with the aim of achieving financial independence before the age of forty-five, preferably forty, and being money-free from an employer. To be able to spend more time with family while they are growing up.

What advice would you give to someone just getting started on their investment journey?
Start by reading some good books. *Millionaire Expat* by Andrew Hallam is what I started with. Getting started is the most important thing. Keep the costs low, you don't need financial advisors/packages that charge you more than 1.5 to 2% per year. Get into the habit of investing early and often, as much as you can comfortably do. Buy all-in-one index funds like Vanguard Target Retirement funds or LifeStrategy funds.

How do you invest?
I use interactive brokers; I buy VWRD (stocks) and IGLO (bonds) with an asset allocation ratio of 90/10.

Which resources (books, online sites, social media feeds, etc.) have you found useful in terms of your investment education?
Books: *Millionaire Expat* by Andrew Hallam, *The Richest Man in Babylon* by George S. Clason, *Think and Grow Rich* by Napoleon Hill.

Instagram: The Expat Investor (although I don't always agree with his portfolio), Personalfinanceclub, StrivewithKristin, Theficouple. Most of these pages are US-focused and really also promote real-estate investing – this is very hard as an expat as you require large deposit amounts, which makes it hard to get involved initially.

Example 4:
Name: Chris Perry
Age: 62
Location: Hong Kong

Why do you invest?
I came to Hong Kong in 1986 as a professional sports coach working for what is now the Hong Kong Sports Institute. Although the salary package was reasonable, there was no form of pension scheme and I realised that I would need to make provision for my future financial security. This is especially the case in the coaching profession, where you are only as good as your last result!

As it happened, I was able to stay in my post for thirty-five years and thus was able to accumulate some significant sums through steady investing.

What advice would you give to someone just getting started on their investment journey?
My main advice would be to start as early as you can and save and invest regularly in low-cost, broad-based index funds or ETFs. Rebalance occasionally and ignore market pundits, dodgy advisors, stock-picking newsletters and people or schemes that offer you above-average returns.

I made quite a few mistakes along the way – the worst being to let an advisor sign me up for a toxic insurance-linked, so-called investment policy. [It] bled my funds for almost ten years before I paid a penalty to get out and never looked back!

How do you invest?

I have a brokerage with Interactive Brokers and have been investing the vast majority of my funds in low-cost index ETFs. I have been doing this for quite a long time now – with a few tweaks to the funds used. Recently, I switched into the Vanguard LifeStrategy 60 UCITS accumulating ETF as an all-in-one solution in Euros – as ultimately I plan to retire in Europe.

I do occasionally dabble in some other types of investment with a strictly limited proportion of my funds (~5%) – this has included options and crypto. I don't kid myself that I am good at this, although I did once make enough with some option trades to buy a Jaguar. I do it for some fun, enjoyment and a bit of education.

My wife (who is Chinese) likes to invest in property and she has proved quite good at that – in typical Chinese style. Buy, sell, rent small apartments; I leave it to her and she seems pretty good at it!

Which resources (books, online sites, social media feeds, etc.) have you found useful in terms of your investment education?

Over the years, I read a huge number of books on investing and subscribed to various newsletters such as The Motley Fool, Blue Chip Growth and so on. Probably spent thousands of dollars! Some educational value but honestly would have been better off investing the money!

The books that made the most impact ultimately were the ones most passive investors end up finding – Andrew Hallam's books, *A Random Walk Down Wall Street*, *The Simple Path to Wealth* by J L Collins etc. I also enjoyed the investing books by Larry E. Swedroe. I have been fortunate to be able to chat with both Andrew and Larry online.

I enjoy a Canadian podcast called the *Rational Reminder* and also the *Bogleheads* podcast hosted by Rick Ferri.

Investing Anti-models

> "The fault, dear Brutus, is not in our stars,
> but in ourselves."

William Shakespeare, Julius Caesar

Society is full of well-educated people who have made foolhardy choices in their lives. This is particularly true in the world of investing. 'Dysrationalia' refers to the inability to think and behave in a rational way, despite sufficient intelligence.

You may have noticed that I used a quote from Isaac Newton at the beginning of the section of the book entitled, 'Standing on the Shoulders of Giants'. Despite his formidable intellectual prowess, Isaac was a hapless investor. Indeed, Newton's investing endeavours can teach us a great deal about how *not* to behave as an investor.

Nassim Nicholas Taleb, author of *The Black Swan*, states:

> "People focus on role models; it is more effective to find anti-models – people you don't want to resemble when you grow up."[98]

So, if the members of FIFI provide us with a series of investing exemplars, or models, then Isaac Newton provides us with an example of an investing anti-model.

What Can Isaac Newton Teach Us About Investing?

A scientist without equal, Newton's accomplishments were vast and speak to an impressive, multi-disciplinary mind. A physicist, a mathematician, an astronomer, but Isaac the investor? How exactly did he fare? To the uninitiated, he would have appeared to possess the profile of a great investor.

Looking back through the rear-view mirror of human history, it is clear to see that this esteemed scientist possessed an imposing, monumental intellect. Naturally, he certainly possessed the inherent analytical capabilities required to make correct decisions, characterised by an obsessive focus on rigorous data and statistical analysis. Isn't this just the recipe for a great investor? Surely, such a great mind would have performed well within the investing domain.

Unfortunately, and of particular misfortune to Mr Newton, this was not the case. As I will now explain, there is a significant difference between being a successful scientist and a successful investor.

In 1720, Newton allowed himself to be swayed by the

---

98   Taleb, Nassim Nicholas, *The Bed of Procrustes: Philosophical and Practical Aphorisms* (Penguin: 2011).

euphoria of other investors and he bought a large number of shares, at an extremely high price, in the South Sea Company – a popular stock at the time in England. Sir Isaac Newton lost £20,000 (an incredibly high amount at the time) when the share price subsequently plummeted.

What lesson can we learn from Sir Isaac Newton's ill-fated investing endeavour? I think we can apply Benjamin Graham's parable of Mr Market when reflecting on Newton's behaviour. Sir Isaac allowed himself to be swayed by the fervour surrounding the stock of the South Sea Company, allowing his emotions to dictate and override his customary rational way of thinking. Benjamin Graham once said, "The investor's chief problem – and even his worst enemy – is likely to be himself." This is certainly true of Sir Isaac Newton and his misfortune with the stock of the South Sea Company.

In this section of the book, I provide examples of common mistakes that can affect investors. It's important for sloth investors to be cognizant of these anti-models, thereby eliminating the potential for themselves to make these very same mistakes.

Investing Anti-model 1 – Misguided Patriotism aka 'Home Bias'

There's often the temptation for some investors to overcommit to their home country's stock market. Within the realm of investing, you'll often hear the phrase 'invest in what you know' (or words to that effect). Consequently, this is something that many of my countrymen (British investors) do. In one sense, it's understandable as there are no doubt psychological factors at play.

Visit your local shopping centre, simply take a look and perhaps observe which shops are busy. Make a note of your observations and then why not invest accordingly? To some, this may appear to be good advice. To purely invest in the businesses of your home country is a mistake, though. Harry, our first anti-model, makes the mistake of overweighting home market stocks in his portfolio.

Harry makes this mistake by ensuring that the sole equity (stock) component of his portfolio is a FTSE 100 ETF tracker. This is an ETF that tracks the FTSE 100 index, an index that essentially contains the 100 largest companies listed on the London Stock Exchange. There will undoubtedly be some great companies contained within this ETF. Harry believes that he knows the companies of his own country and is therefore well qualified to assess the quality of these companies.

However, why should Harry restrict himself to purely investing in the largest one hundred companies in his home country of the UK? Harry fails to appreciate that there's a big, wide world out there with innovative companies spanning the globe. By solely investing in a FTSE 100 ETF tracker, he is disregarding the potential for his money to grow by being invested in the most prominent countries (and companies) from around the world.

Also, as I explained in the earlier section 'Own the World', there's the potential for home bias to have truly disastrous effects, especially if the stock market of your home country performs particularly poorly.

Again, it's worth reflecting on the performance of the Japanese stock market here. Many years of high returns in the immediate post-war period compelled a significant number of Japanese investors to become complacent and succumb to home bias. This was a mistake because in 1990 the Japanese benchmark index, the Nikkei 225, plunged by more than 60% and hasn't recovered since.

An additional point to add and one that I also referred to in the section, 'Own the World', is that the British stock market represents around 4% of the global stock market. Accordingly, if you check out the fact sheet for a globally diversified ETF from a provider such as Vanguard, you will note that around 4% of this fund's assets are allocated to the United Kingdom.

The Sloth Investor does not deny the fact that there will always be national stock markets that outperform a globally diversified index. However, due to the absence of a crystal ball, how can we be sure which countries these will be (and for how long?)?

Rather than overweighting the equity component of his portfolio to the UK, the better, more rational strategy for Harry would be to simply invest in a low-fee, globally diversified ETF that tracks a global index.

Investing Anti-model 2 – Making Decisions Based on Economic Forecasts

My second anti-model is the investor that makes decisions based on economic forecasts. At first glance, the motive is understandable. After all, as human beings, we crave certainty, but, as investors, we must always remember that uncertainty is the only certainty.

Within the realm of investing, forecasting is very common. However, unlike the weather, accurate economic forecasts are incredibly difficult to formulate. As Niall Ferguson, the financial historian, states in his 2021 book, *Doom*, the economic system has been increasingly complex since the industrial revolution.[99]

This is something that Fiona, our second anti-model, fails to appreciate. Fiona is consistently keen to obtain an 'edge' by reading varied forecasts in the financial section of her favourite newspaper and following financial pundits on X (formerly Twitter). However, the absence of the proverbial crystal ball means that it's incredibly difficult to accurately gauge the trajectory of the stock market.

So, instead of attempting to imitate Nostradamus, what should Fiona seek to do? Fiona should simply adhere to simplicity, the first bedrock principle of the sloth investor. Tune out the noise, disregard the soundbite circus of the financial media and consistently invest month after month, whether the stock market is moving up or whether it is moving down.

Investing Anti-model 3 – Demonstrating a Lack of Patience

As I referred to in the section of the book devoted to being headstrong – the fifth bedrock principle of the sloth investor

---

99 Ferguson, Niall, *Doom: The Politics of Catastrophe* (Penguin Press: 2021).

– recency bias is something that can throw investors off track and, perhaps, deter many people from even getting started on their investing journey.

Recency bias refers to the tendency for people to attach great significance to recent events and place less emphasis on events that have occurred in the past. Confronted with difficult decisions, particularly during times of volatility, humans – i.e. investors – like to take shortcuts. After all, with the absence of the proverbial crystal ball, doesn't it seem easier to naturally reference what's taken place most recently – i.e. think in the short term by placing our faith in recent events?

However, as you know by now, thinking in the long term is a prerequisite of the sloth investor. Taking a long-term approach is easier said than done, though. From an evolutionary perspective, our brains are hardwired for the short term. In our role as hunter-gatherers, foraging for food and seeking to avoid death, humans' commitment to the short term ensured survival.

The paradox here, though, is that while an intense focus on the short term ensured survival for our primordial ancestors, an intense focus on the short term for investors could have fatal consequences for your finances.

So, at this point, let's take a look at Spencer, our third anti-model. Spencer is twenty-three years old. He's a recent university graduate and he's landed a position in a respectable company. Spencer's earning well and he's committed to allocating a sizable chunk of his monthly salary towards investing. He's starting his investing journey at the turn of 2020. Spencer read much about the impressive returns of the overall stock market in the prior decade and is keen to capitalise on the returns of this wealth-generating machine. Consequently, he decided to invest in a low-fee, globally diversified ETF.

But wait… things don't go entirely according to plan for Spencer. Covid-19 began its rapid spread and there's a stock market crash in March of that year. On Monday 9th March, the Dow Jones fell 2,014 points – a drop of 7.79%. Three days later, on Thursday 12th March, the index fell a further 2,352 points, dropping 9.99%. Four days later, on Monday 16th March, the Dow sank by nearly 3,000 points, losing 12.9%.

Now, can you imagine how investors around the world were feeling? Panic gripped the minds of many, including Spencer. A young, inexperienced investor, the scale of the declines was too much for him. On his daily commute to and from work during those days, he read numerous sensationalist headlines and, by mid-March, he had enough. Fearing continual, never-ending declines as a consequence of projecting the short term into the long term, Spencer took the decision to terminate his investing career. Yes, that's right, Spencer allowed recency bias to overwhelm his own best interests.

As, by now, you've no doubt recognised, a better course of action for Spencer would have been to remain inactive – i.e. by simply doing nothing with his portfolio. However, the combination of recency bias and a bias towards action compelled Spencer to bring an abrupt end to his investing career.

So, what's the remedy for the type of behaviour that Spencer demonstrated? After all, none of us possess a crystal ball. Yes, while none of us possess a crystal ball, we can strive to possess a good understanding of market history, develop an appreciation for the biases that have afflicted so many investors in the past and finally recognise the virtue of remaining inactive – a central tenet of the sloth investor that I have sought to reaffirm again and again throughout this book.

It's interesting to note that in April of 2020, the market started to rebound. Had Spencer been in possession of the above three traits, it's likely that he would have remained invested rather than throwing in the towel at such a young age. One can only now imagine the opportunity cost of Spencer's decision, of not being a participant in the forward march of the market.

Investing Anti-model 4 – Allowing 'Ingroup Bias' to Deter You from Investing

A young man named Steve is our fourth anti-model. He's just turned eighteen years old and recently a financial writer visited his school to deliver a presentation on investing. With little prior knowledge of investing (neither of his parents has ever invested), Steve's ears pricked up when he heard the speaker discuss the wonders of compound interest and the long-term, historical returns of the stock market.

Later that week, he raised the subject of the presentation with his parents. However, soon after mentioning the realm of investing to his parents, Steve's initial enthusiasm dampened. His parents promptly informed him that investing is gambling and that 'it's not something he should be bothered about'.

Steve is loyal to his parents, inherently believing that they have his best interests at heart and so he favours their opinion over that of the financial writer. In this regard, Steve is demonstrating something known as 'ingroup bias'. This refers to our tendency to favour the views and beliefs of people that belong within one's own group.

Of course, this is only natural. From an evolutionary perspective, it was historically the best, most functional course of action for humans to view members of other groups as potentially harmful. Forming a clear distinction between 'them' and 'us' enabled humans to avert danger.

Despite the evolutionary advantages of this form of behaviour, rigidly adhering to the advice of his parents is undoubtedly going to impose a tremendous cost on Steve's ability to grow his money over time.

Investing Anti-model 5 – Authority Bias and the Hazards It Can Bring

For our final investing anti-model, let me introduce you to Casper. Casper is an expatriate who has freshly arrived in the Middle East courtesy of being offered a teaching position at an international school in the region. For the sake of clarity, let's say that Casper is a young British man (in his twenties) and he will be working in Dubai.

Expatriate workers, working away from their home country, are often subject to a reduction in the number of financial products that they have access to. Quite simply, one's status as an expatriate will invariably mean that your ability to use the investment brokerages in your home country may be significantly reduced, if not altogether taken away (this is often the most likely scenario, due to reasons of taxation).

However, despite the fact that the investment options for expatriates may be reduced, there are still ways that they can invest their hard-earned money.

First of all, though, there are some hurdles that need to be overcome. That's right, expatriates must be sure to avoid the potential perils that other expatriates have succumbed to in the past.

The Dangers of Authority Bias

Having worked away from my home country (the UK) for over a decade, I've been dismayed by the countless individuals I've spoken to who have been charmed and then, subsequently, dismayed by sharp-suited, jargon-filled 'financial professionals'.

It's perhaps not difficult to see how this could happen. After all, let's take a look at the common features of such 'financial professionals', features that can often bewitch and beguile new investors. Commonly, they will be an employee of an organisation with a regal sounding name and invariably they'll be clutching a glossy company brochure that they'll be keen to share with you. Here are some other features that we can associate with such individuals:

- A smart suit
- A briefcase
- The utterance of a significant amount of jargon

The final point, the deliberately opaque vocabulary that they use, is particularly important as it convinces many expats that the field of investing is too complex and too encumbered with jargon for them to comprehend. This is, of course, exactly what these financial professionals want expatriates to think. You may recall how in the section of the book on 'Low Fees', I referred to the 'conspiracy against the laity' and how the use of complex language leaves many people to believe that investing is too difficult for them.

Okay, so I may be accused of serving up a stereotype, but the simple fact is that many expatriates in the past have fallen prey to the sharp-suited 'financial professionals' that I have just described.

Impression Amplifiers

A smart suit, a briefcase, financial jargon... the Sloth Investor refers to these elements as 'impression amplifiers'. You could say that the deployment of such elements, on the part of a financial professional, is akin to a peacock spreading its feathers and flexing its prowess. Therefore, it's easy to see how these elements or 'impression amplifiers', as I like to call them, could cause a new investor to part with their hard-earned money.

These impression amplifiers function as agents of persuasion. Quite simply, we engender our trust in these so-called authority figures. This is because human beings naturally possess an inclination towards something known as 'authority bias'. Authority bias refers to the tendency for people to confer special privilege and respect to the decision-making of individuals that they deem to be in a position of authority. Authority bias compels many expats to outsource their investments to the representatives of financial services companies.

Nightmare on Expat Street – Avoid the Predatory Sharks!

Let's circle back now to Casper, our fresh-off-the-plane young British expatriate. A combination of factors makes many expatriates (both British and non-British) easy prey to the predatory sharks that often circle the financial waters overseas. Here are a few characteristics that could potentially describe expatriates, thus making them an attractive sight to financial professionals overseas.

- The availability of more disposable income than they were accustomed to in their home country.
- An inability to use regulated financial institutions back home due to their expatriate status.
- A lack of investment experience (perhaps even the presence of an inner 'imposter syndrome'), leading them to entrust their faith in the financial professionals that they may encounter internationally.

These characteristics make expatriates prey to the predatory sharks (financial professionals) that commonly circulate in international waters (this has been a particular problem for expatriates in the Middle East).

Andrew Hallam, the aforementioned author of *Millionaire Teacher* and *Millionaire Expat* refers to these financial professionals as 'snakes in suits'.[100]

Unfortunately, as you might expect by now, these financial professionals don't necessarily have your best interests in mind. This is because the products recommended by these 'professionals' are usually high-fee, actively managed, poor performing and incredibly difficult to extricate oneself from. Although it's already been stated within this book, it's a point well worth reiterating that despite their consistent bold, potent claims of outperformance, financial professionals are commonly undeserving of the claim of 'professional'. In an article entitled, 'The Loser's Game', Charles D. Ellis states:

> "The investment-management business (it should be a profession but is not) is built upon a simple and basic belief: Professional money managers can beat the market. That premise appears to be false."[101]

Despite the evidence in favour of a passive approach to investing, many British expatriates (in addition to other nationalities) have succumbed to the sharp-talking allure of the purveyors of actively managed funds. Writing in *Millionaire Expat – How to Build Wealth Living Overseas*, author Andrew Hallam states:

---

100 'Millionaire Expat Shakes Up Snakes In' by Andrew Hallam. Published September 13 2017 [https://andrewhallam.com/millionaire-expat-shakes-up-snakes-in-suits/].

101 'The Loser's Game' by Charles D. Ellis. Published in *Financial Analysts Journal*, 1975.

"Investing with actively managed funds is like walking
up a downward-heading escalator. Those doing so
fight more than gravity. But many expats face the same
daunting task with 80-pound rucksacks… they're
sold debilitating offshore pensions, otherwise known
as investment-linked assurance schemes (ILASs)…
advisors selling such products can earn commissions
high enough to make a cadaver blush. Investors buying
them get stiffed. The investments are usually portfolios
of actively managed mutual funds coupled with an
insurance component. Neither the investment nor the
insurance is typically worth the money."[102]

Unfortunately, Casper, our fictitious young British expatriate and our fifth anti-model, is one such individual who allows himself to be deceived into signing up for one of the schemes that Andrew Hallam expertly describes above. Having little prior knowledge of investing, soon after arriving in Dubai he is enticed by a sharp-talking 'snake in a suit' and naively signs up for a high-fee, investment-linked assurance scheme that really will not work in his best interest. If only Casper had been made aware of the bedrock principles of a sloth investor – i.e. implementing an investment strategy that is defined by investing in a low-fee, globally diversified manner.

Low-fee ETFs/Index Funds Are Kryptonite For Financial Professionals

Interestingly, when I asked some of my expatriate friends how these active fund aficionados ('professional money

102 Hallam, Andrew. *Millionaire Expat: How to Build Wealth Living Overseas* (2nd ed.), (Wiley: 2018).

managers' located abroad) reacted when they mentioned low-fee index funds/ETFs to them, they told me that these 'financial professionals' were reluctant to enter into a conversation with them concerning these low-fee funds.

Indeed, it's not uncommon for many of these financial professionals to delicately pirouette questions about costs when their potential customers seek to pursue such a rational, entirely reasonable line of enquiry. The reason is that the low-fee structure of index fund trackers is an inconvenient truth for many financial professionals. Indeed, the mere mention of index funds is their equivalent form of kryptonite.

So, How Can I Invest as an Expatriate?

As I've mentioned, one's status as an expatriate will most likely prohibit that person from accessing the same degree of investment options that their home-based compatriots will have access to. Despite this fact, expatriates can still apply the same principles of investing in a low-fee, globally diversified ETF that tracks a global index.

Just as they would in their domestic country, expatriates can purchase a low-fee, globally diversified ETF and a bond ETF (should you wish to incorporate bonds within your portfolio) by using an international (sometimes known as 'offshore') brokerage.

Within Chapter 11, I'll also provide additional information that will be of support to expatriate investors.

Ten Questions a Sloth Investor May Have

1. What is the difference between an index fund and an ETF?

Okay, so let's begin with ETFs. Firstly, let me explain that the term 'ETF' is an abbreviation for 'exchange-traded fund'.

Quite simply, ETFs are collections of stocks, bonds and/ or other investment types that you can buy, just like you buy an individual company stock.

So, let's say you're interested in capturing the growth that's taking place among the largest, most notable companies in the United States. You could purchase an ETF that tracks the S&P 500 index. However, let's now remind ourselves what the S&P 500 index is.

The S&P 500 is an index that contains the five hundred largest publicly traded US companies. When you hear the word index, you may likely think of an index at the back of a non-fiction book containing significant, notable words from the book that are organised alphabetically.

So, likewise, because I think it's a point worth repeating again, the S&P 500 index contains the most significant, most notable companies in the US – i.e. the five hundred largest publicly traded companies.

Fortunately, you don't have to buy all of those stocks individually. That would, of course, be incredibly time-consuming and also a little crazy. Instead, you could simply just purchase an S&P 500 ETF.

Okay, so let me explain the differences between an ETF and index fund, as even though they are similar, it's important to be clear about the distinct differences.

An ETF and an index fund are very similar. For example, invariably you'll find that an S&P 500 ETF will hold the same five hundred stocks that are contained within the S&P 500 index. That's a key reason why ETFs are sometimes referred to as tracker funds. They simply track the composition of stocks and the underlying performance of their benchmark index.

Vanguard's S&P 500 index fund holds the same five hundred stocks that the iShares S&P 500 ETF holds. So, in this regard, they're very similar.

However, let's move on to the differences. A key difference is that the manner of purchasing an index fund and an ETF differs. You buy index funds directly from a fund company. In contrast, investors generally purchase ETFs directly from a stock exchange through a brokerage.

Also, an ETF trades just like a stock on a stock exchange

and this therefore explains the 'exchange-traded' in their name. The price of an ETF will change throughout the trading day, with orders being executed very quickly while the stock market is open for trading.

An index fund, on the other hand, is different. An index fund is priced just once a day, after the market closes. At that point, any orders placed during the day will be executed.

2. Why haven't you mentioned cryptocurrencies, such as Bitcoin?

Cryptocurrencies have garnered a lot of attention in recent years. The most widely accepted cryptocurrency (and the first) is Bitcoin. The Sloth Investor is distinctly not a fan of cryptocurrencies. I'll now explain why.

Let's consider one of the essential features of stocks of the many varied businesses that you invest in when you purchase a low-fee, globally diversified index or ETF. The businesses that are solidly managed will create cash and the really amazing companies generate lots of the stuff (think Apple, Microsoft et al.).

Conversely, cryptocurrencies such as Bitcoin do not generate cash. Quite simply, a cryptocurrency, be it Bitcoin or another iteration, is only worth as much as the market wants to pay. It's notable that in an interview with CNBC in 2014, Warren Buffett was particularly dismissive of the notion of Bitcoin and other cryptocurrencies being viable investments.[103]

---

103 'Buffett Blasts Bitcoin as "Mirage": "Stay Away!"' by Alex Crippen. Published on CNBC on 14th March 2014 – [cnbc. com/2014/03/14/buffett-blasts-bitcoin-as-mirage-stay-away.html].

3. Who could support me to set up my own sloth investment portfolio?

Okay, so let's say that you're keen to begin constructing your sloth investor portfolio, but you still require a little bit of extra support. Perhaps you're feeling nervous about the process of getting started and would be grateful for some additional guidance. If that's the case, there is someone who can help.

Do you remember the second bedrock principle of the sloth investor? That's right, it's low fees. By now, you should know that the sloth investor is consistently keen to keep the cost of investing as low as possible. However, the sloth investor recognises that there will be occasions when some individuals require extra support and, in such circumstances, the sloth investor believes that is perfectly understandable and acceptable to pay a one-off fee to an advisor to support you in setting up a low-fee, globally diversified portfolio.

The Mark of a Good Advisor? Instructing You How to Construct a Simple, Low-fee, Globally Diversified Portfolio

Mark Zoril is a godsend for newbie investors. The reason is that he supports investors in setting up their own portfolio of low-fee, globally diversified index funds. Remember my disdain for financial professionals from earlier on? Well, with this particular financial professional (Mark Zoril), it's important to make a clear distinction. While many financial professionals invest their client's money, Mark Zoril teaches his clients how to get set up on their own.

Does the Sloth Investor Know Mark Zoril Personally?

At this stage, you may be wondering whether there's any professional affiliation between Mark Zoril and the Sloth Investor. For example, would I potentially receive a commission if a new client of Mark's mentions that they've read *The Sloth Investor*?

The answer is a resounding '*no*'. The simple reason why Mark Zoril merits inclusion in this book is because I personally have numerous close friends that have utilised Mark's service and each one has spoken positively about the support that he provided them with.

At the current time of writing, PlanVision charges $239 for their service of helping you to get set up with your own low-fee, globally diversified portfolio. If you feel that you are someone who would benefit from speaking to Mark, then you'll find his contact details below.

Email: markzoril@planvisionmn.com
Tel: 1-855-965-4286
Website: https://planvisionmn.com/expats/

4.   *Should I invest a lump sum amount of money all at once?*

It's generally the case that most investors in the stock market will invest on a monthly or quarterly basis. This is known as dollar cost averaging (DCA). Investing in this way, with a consistent, standard sum of money, ensures that the investor purchases more shares when prices are low and fewer shares when prices are high.

However, let's say that you're fortunate to have become the beneficiary of a large sum of money. Whether this be a bonus payment/gratuity from work, a gift from a family member or from some other source, you're naturally keen to know more about whether to invest it all at once or to spread the lump sum amount over a series of monthly/quarterly investments.

Psychology plays a key role in such circumstances. For instance, let's say that you decide to invest the entire lump sum and the very next day the stock market plunges 25%. How do you think you would feel? If you think that you could handle this, then you should likely opt for the lump-sum investment all at once.

Interestingly, there are several findings that lend weight to the odds being in your favour of investing a lump sum amount all at once, as opposed to investing the amount on a monthly or quarterly basis. In 2012, Vanguard published a study[104] that demonstrated that investing a lump sum, as soon as you acquire it, will usually beat dollar-cost averaging.

In support of this, University of Connecticut finance professors John R. Knight and Lewis Mandell were responsible for a study in 1993 that spanned a variety of time periods and found that investing a lump sum upfront outperformed dollar cost averaging most of the time.[105]

---

104 'Dollar-Cost Averaging Just Means Taking Risk Later' by Anatoly Shtekhman, Christos Tasopoulos and Brian Wimmer. Published by Vanguard Research, July 2012. – [static.twentyoverten.com/5980d16bbfb1c93238ad9c24/rJpQmY8o7/Dollar-Cost-Averaging-Just-Means-Taking-Risk-Later-Vanguard.pdf].

105 'Nobody Gains from Dollar Cost Averaging: Analytical, Numerical and Empirical Results' by John R. Knight and Lewis Mandell. Published in Financial Services Review 2 (1): 51–61 (1993) – [citeseerx.ist.psu.edu/viewdoc/download?doi=10.1.1.320.2252&rep=rep1&type=pdf].

5. Which ETF provider should I use?

Throughout this book I've waxed lyrical about Vanguard. While it's true that Mr Sloth is a huge admirer of the company's founder, the late John C Bogle, the truth is that it doesn't really make much difference which fund provider you use. On their official company websites, fund providers will provide the fees for each of their funds. This is certainly true of companies such as Vanguard, iShares and Schwab.

Whether you're buying a low-fee, globally diversified ETF from Vanguard, iShares or Schwab, the simple fact is that each fund will be almost identical in composition. Don't sweat the small stuff. Just get started!

6. What should I do if I find a cheaper ETF?

Okay, so this question naturally follows on from Question 5. It's important to be aware of the fact that new ETFs are continually being launched. So, let's say that when you begin investing you opted for a low-fee, globally diversified ETF that charges 0.14% per year for every $10,000 invested (resulting in a total fee of $14). Then, a year later, an alternative fund provider introduces a new, low-fee globally diversified ETF that costs 0.11% per year. Investing in this fund would cost $11 for every $10,000 invested. The question you have to ask yourself is whether it is truly necessary to worry and fret about a possible saving of $3? Also, who knows, perhaps the ETF that is currently charging 0.14% per year may reduce their fees the following year.

Rather than overthinking relatively small-scale changes like this, it's important to maintain a firm grip on the bigger picture, which is to consistently invest by adhering to each of the sloth investor's five bedrock principles. Again, don't sweat the small stuff!

7. *Should I wait until the geopolitical climate is calmer before I begin investing?*

Oh, so you possess a crystal ball? Well, lucky you. Hey, if you don't mind, could I borrow it once you have finished with it?

Seriously, though, when isn't there geopolitical strife? As I've described previously in this book, sloth investors invest through the good times and the bad. Waiting for a 'calmer' geopolitical climate suggests that one has a crystal ball and is suggestive of market timing.

Don't try to play a guessing game. Whether the market is at all-time highs or all-time lows, you just need to remember to consistently invest in a low-fee, passive manner, in a globally diversified ETF/index fund.

8. *What's likely to be the biggest obstacle to my success as an investor?*

Okay, dear reader, I may surprise you now, but I'm going to avoid talking about psychology and how you react to markets and tense geopolitical moments etc. Throughout this book, I've spoken at length about these facets of your life as an investor.

Instead, I'm going to go back to basics and focus on your savings rate. After all, how can you expect to generate a considerable investment portfolio if you are unable to get into the habit of regularly setting aside a consequential amount of your income/salary for the purposes of investment?

It doesn't matter which particular ETF or ETF fund provider you opt for if you are unable to get your spending habits under control. A small disclosure for you now. In an earlier iteration of this book, I had intended to create a 'Money Sense' section, but for the sake of simplicity (and, dear reader, your own time), I decided to omit that section.

However, let me just take the time now to urge you to get a good handle on your spending. Got a subscription you're not using anymore? Get rid of it! Eating out for lunch every day? That's way too much; make yourself lunch at least several times a week (if not more).

I could go on, but I'd like to echo a point made to me by Nikki Dunn (an advocate for women in finance and financial literacy) in episode twenty-six of *The Sloth Investor* podcast. Nikki mentioned the concept of 'cash flow clarity', meaning the importance of becoming truly clear and cognizant about how exactly your cash is being deployed.

The Importance of Experiences

At this point during this foray into money matters, I'd like to highlight the importance of experiences. In episode thirteen of *The Sloth Investor* podcast, my co-host, Jason, and I spoke about how experiences, not things, make humans happy.

During our discussion, we frequently referenced the

research that supports this notion, which is contained in the book, *Happy Money – The Science of Happier Spending* by Elizabeth Dunn and Michael Norton.[106] In the book, the authors cite the work of Travis Carter and Tom Gilovich, two US-based researchers. Carter and Gilovich asked undergraduates to write a summary of their life story and they discovered that these students were more likely to mention experiential purchases, rather than material goods.

The name of the study is 'I am what I do, not what I have' and it was published in the *Journal of Personality and Social Psychology* in February 2012. I've included the final two sentences from that piece of research below as I think they're pretty powerful:

> "Our memories are what make us who we are. If we make purchases that contribute to our sense of self – that is, if we pursue experiences over material goods – there are likely to be more memories, more of us, to cherish and embrace."[107]

9. Do you have any recommended resources?

Naturally, I have to begin with *The Sloth Investor* podcast, which you'll find on my Sloth Investor YouTube channel. There, you'll find every episode of my podcast, investment book reviews and other content related to investing like a sloth.

---

106 Dunn, Elizabeth and Norton, Michael, *Happy Money: The Science of Happier Spending* (Simon and Schuster: 2014).

107 Carter, T. J. and Gilovich, T., 'I am what I do, not what I have: The differential centrality of experiential and material purchases to the self'. *Journal of Personality and Social Psychology*, *102*(6), 1304–1317 – [doi.org/10.1037/a0027407].

Books:

The Sloth Investor is a compound creation of the numerous books that I have read about investing. There are too many to list, but here are a selection of my favourites:

- *The Psychology of Money* by Morgan Housel
- *A Wealth of Common Sense* by Ben Carlson
- *The Behavioral Investor* by Daniel Crosby
- *The Geometry of Wealth* by Brian Portnoy
- *The Power of Passive Investing* by Richard Ferri
- *Enough* by John C Bogle
- *Invest Your Way to Financial Freedom* by Ben Carlson & Robin Powell
- *The Simple Path to Wealth* by J L Collins

Other:

- Morgan Housel's blog[108] – Morgan Housel is, quite simply, my favourite investment writer. His blog pieces are extremely well written and the success of his book, *The Psychology of Money* (listed above), is testament to his skills as a writer.
- Robin Powell is a tireless advocate for index fund investing in the UK. You can follow him on X (formerly Twitter) at @RobinJPowell and his blog[109] is crammed full of helpful videos and articles, and is a great resource for investors (particularly those based in the UK).

---

108 See: [collabfund.com/blog/authors/morgan].
109 See: [evidenceinvestor.com/home-uk].

10. How can I cultivate my child's financial literacy?

Talking about money from a young age with your children is crucial. Indeed, a study by Cambridge University[110] found that children are already able to grasp basic money concepts between the ages of three and four. However, according to a 2018 survey by T. Rowe Price[111], only 4% of parents said they started discussing financial topics with their kids before the age of five.

In addition to talking to your children about money, books are a great way to enable children to learn more about finance. Within the last few years, there have been several great financially oriented books for kids. These include:

- *M is for Money* by Rob Phelan: this fantastic book, designed for children aged three to eight years old, presents a range of financial terms, in the form of an ABC of Money book. If you want to learn more about how this book was conceived, then I encourage you to listen to episode twenty-three of *The Sloth Investor* podcast, in which I interviewed the author.

- *Grandpa's Fortune Fables: Fun Stories to Teach Kids About Money* by Will Rainey. This book caters to an

---

110 Whitebread, Dr David and Bingham, Dr Sue, *Habit Formation and Learning in Young Children*, The Money Advice Service. Published by the Money Advice Service, 2013 – [mascdn.azureedge.net/cms/ the-money-advice-service-habit-formation-and-learning-in-young-children-may2013.pdf].

111 T Rowe Price, *10th Annual Parents, Kids & Money Survey* (March 2018) – [slideshare.net/TRowePrice/t-rowe-prices-10th-annual-parents-kids-money-survey].

older audience than the previous title. It features a thirteen-year-old girl named Gail who hears about her grandpa's adventures to a faraway island, where he learned how to look after his money and become a very wealthy man.

Conclusion

"Investors should remember that their scorecard is not
computed using Olympic diving methods: Degree-of-
difficulty doesn't count."

Warren Buffett's letter to Berkshire Hathaway Shareholders, 1994

I happened to begin writing this, the concluding section of
The Sloth Investor, during the closing ceremony of the Tokyo
2020 Olympics, which, of course, were rescheduled to the
summer months of 2021.

Now that you're reading the final stages of the book, I
thought it may be interesting to consider these concluding
words to be the equivalent of the closing ceremony for *The
Sloth Investor*. After all, there are useful parallels that can be
drawn between the world of track and field and investing.

It's a Marathon, Not a Sprint!

I was fortunate to be in London during the 2012 Olympics and
two athletes that shone during this particular Olympiad were
Usain Bolt and Mo Farah. Bolt triumphantly trounced all of his
rivals over a short distance and Mo Farah captured the hearts of
millions of Brits with his heroic, long-distance feats.

As you know by now, Mr Sloth's investing philosophy is underpinned by a belief in five bedrock principles, with 'time' being one of them. Therefore, one of the chief aims of this book was to make it clear to you that investing should be considered to be a *marathon*, not a sprint (sorry, Mr Bolt).

As you know, varied factors affected the stability of the stock market during the investment life cycle of 'ordinary' investors such as Grace Groner. A world war, the world possibly ending (the Cuban Missile Crisis), a presidential assassination, an oil crisis, 9/11... I could go on. All of these events could (and probably did) compel many people to stop investing and to pull their money from the stock market. However, what sets extraordinary investors like Grace Groner apart is their ability to weather the storm and remain on track within their investment journey by continuing to invest through thick and thin.

Likewise, a sloth investor recognises that the periodic bouts of volatility that intermittently affect the stock market are simply an inherent feature of one's life as an investor. Consequently, a sloth investor remains invested through good times and bad, demonstrating the steadfast ability to always remain invested, thereby adhering to the bedrock principle of time. Critically, a sloth investor instinctively recognises that successful investing is akin to a marathon, not a sprint.

The Curious (but Reliable) Coil of the Capital Markets

Okay, so Mr Sloth doesn't know much about the shot put, but he does know that a crucial element of a successful shot put throw is the 'torso coil'. This is the term that is used to describe the torso rotation that professional shot putters undertake. The image of a coil is a useful one for investors to refer to during a sustained market decline – i.e. like the global financial crisis of 2008.

We can picture a spring coil being fully compressed as it goes down. However, the more it goes down, the more powerful the force that there will be to subsequently thrust it back to normal levels. If you happen to be reading this book during the period of a sustained market decline, you may find it useful to consider this analogy.

Be Mentally Strong!

Olga Korbut, Belarusian gymnast and four-time Olympic gold medallist, had this to say about her success: "This ability to conquer oneself is no doubt the most precious of all things sports bestows."

I like this quote because of its relevance to the field of investing. As I stated at the beginning of the section on 'Headstrong', the fifth bedrock principle of the sloth investor, an individual doesn't need to look far to encounter what is likely to be the biggest obstacle to their success as an investor: themself!

Having read about the cognitive biases discussed in Chapter 5, have you taken the time to reflect upon your own patterns of thinking? Moreover, it's important to be mindful of the effect that the rapid twists and turns of the stock market can exert on our minds. Ruminating on the natural back and forth of the stock market will do nothing but erode your ability to be a successful investor. Sloth investors are cognizant of this, ensuring that they don't react with wild excitement to new market highs, but nor do they succumb to the groupthink pessimism that can rear its ugly head during times of market turmoil.

In essence, sloth investors are prepared for both swings of the pendulum – i.e. the euphoric highs and the ever-so gloomy lows. So, the ability to remain level-headed reaps great reward for both the athlete and the investor.

The Sloth Investor Hall of Fame

With sixteen gold medals between them, there's no doubt in my mind that the aforementioned Olympians Olga Korbut, Usain Bolt and Mo Farah belong in the Olympic Hall of Fame. Indeed, in 1988, Olga became the first inductee into the International Gymnastics Hall of Fame. As I begin to bring this Olympic-themed conclusion to a close, let me take this opportunity to remind you about the gold medal merits of investing luminaries such as Warren Buffett and Jack Bogle.

I consider Bogle, Buffett and the other investors that I discussed in Chapters 2 and 3 to be the inaugural inductees into the 'Sloth Investor Hall of Fame'. In fact, you can hear me wax lyrical about their influence on the sloth investor's investing philosophy within my podcast series, available via YouTube, Spotify and Apple Podcasts (Jack Bogle is featured in episode ten and Warren Buffett is featured in episode fifteen).

You can learn a great deal from the investors that I featured at the beginning of this book. I know I certainly did. As we come into the home straight of this book, the Sloth Investor once again encourages you to stand upon the metaphorical shoulders of these investing giants.

The Spirit of *Philotimo*

The Olympic tradition, of course, descends from Ancient Greece. In Chapter 3, I mentioned that I love the study of etymology – the study of words and their origins. Therefore, it is perhaps fitting that in the concluding section of this book, I use a Greek term to encourage you, the reader, to pass on the lessons that you have learned from what you have read.

The English language is great, but the combination of a wide reading habit and my time working abroad has enabled me to acquire knowledge of a varied assortment of multicultural phrases that I love. One such phrase is *philotimo*. *Philotimo* is Greek in origin and means to be of service, to focus on assisting others.

Several of the individuals I have mentioned in this book embody the 'Spirit of *Philotimo*'. Perhaps most notably, Andrew Hallam is a key example. Indeed, it's naturally easy to mention the notion of *philotimo* (this idea of being of service) and Andrew Hallam in the same breath. Let's take a look at the evidence.

The authorship of several investment books, an investment-themed website and investing workshops, Andrew Hallam has exemplified *philotimo* through all of these endeavours. I am a direct beneficiary of the books that he has written about investing. The same can be said about many other investors around the world.

Inoculate Others Against Financial Illiteracy – Pass the Sloth Investment Baton On!

After reading this book, I strongly encourage you also to engage in the spirit of *philotimo* yourself and being of service to others by spreading what you have learned about the merits of adopting an inactive, index approach to investing – i.e. behaving like a sloth investor.

Too many people suffer from a disease known as investment illiteracy. Of course, I jest, but, in all seriousness, I never cease to be amazed by the lack of investment sense that afflicts many people. What's the best method of inoculation against such financial folly? A strong dose of *philotimo*.

Deploying yet another athletic analogy, I strongly urge you to pass the 'investment baton' on to others. Knowledge such as this has an incredible compounding effect. Be of service, spread the word, start today!

Don't Sacrifice an Investment in Your Future Self

Originally, the Olympics were a religious festival. In fact, historically, the centrepiece at the Olympics was not a sporting event, but a sacrifice. On day three of the games, one hundred oxen would be sacrificed and burnt in the presence of the athletes.

So, what connection is there between the concept of 'sacrifice' and the realm of investing? Well, I would argue that a failure to invest means that you are sacrificing the potential of your future self. Linking back to Chapter 4 of this book, I wrote within that chapter of how investing can broaden one's life options. Please do not lose sight of this important fact.

It's incredibly important to recognise that investing your income in a wise, rational and sloth-like manner can function as a choice enabler, widening the possibility for enriching your opportunities and life experiences.

Keep It Simple, Sloth!

There can be no doubt about the gruelling degree of sacrifice and commitment required to be a successful Olympic athlete. As I noted at the beginning of this book, Malcolm Gladwell, in his landmark book, *Outliers*, argued that 10,000 hours of sustained practice should be considered to be the rule of thumb for an individual to become an expert in their field. Citing the Beatles' early performance career in Hamburg, Germany, as an example, Gladwell certainly makes a compelling case for the correlation between sustained, deliberate practice and greatness.

Despite this claim, let me make it clear to you again that *it does not take 10,000 hours of practice to be a great investor*. As I hope it became clear to you in Chapter 5, in the section on being 'Headstrong', the sloth investor recognises that the overapplication of one's mental powers can, in fact, cause mistakes to be made.

An appreciation for simplicity, the first bedrock principle of the sloth investor, is once again worth reminding ourselves about. I'm fond of the quote by Warren Buffett that I used at the beginning of this conclusion. The reason is because it once again underlines the importance of recognising the key role that *simplicity* can play in shaping your approach to investing.

While there may be a significant degree of complexity and time involved in an Olympic athlete's training, whether they be diver, gymnast, triathlete or rower, the approach required by the sloth investor is underscored by simplicity. Quite simply, you can dismiss any thought of 10,000 hours of deliberate practice. Instead, you, the sloth investor, need to be deliberately sloth-like.

The humble sloth, with its lethargic behaviour, undoubtedly does not possess the necessary credentials required to be an Olympic athlete. However, in the field of investing, a podium finish becomes a very realistic result, indeed worthy of a standing ovation.

Acknowledgements

I am deeply grateful to all those individuals who have, in their own unique way, shaped the creation of *The Sloth Investor*.

Firstly, thank you to the team at Troubador. Your support and guidance during each step of the production process was vital, thereby enabling this book to come into being.

Let me also doff my hat (can sloths even wear hats?) to each of the members of FIFI, the five international fantasy investors that I mentioned in Chapter 3 of this book. The influence of Jack Bogle, Warren Buffett, Benjamin Graham, Morgan Housel, and Robin Powell played a significant role in the formation of my five bedrock principles.

From the above stellar quintet, a special mention must be attributed to the late, great Jack Bogle, an absolute titan of intellectual discourse on investment and the figure responsible for creating the approach to investing that I advocate throughout this book. My respect for Jack Bogle is incalculable. Oceans of ink have been spilt on Warren Buffett, but in my humble opinion not enough has been written (nor enough credit given) to the immeasurable influence of the late Mr Bogle.

Given my quest to simplify investing and to enable my readers to recognise that anyone can invest, I would also like to give credit to the influence of the teacher (Andrew Hallam), the mechanic (Russ Perry) and the secretary (Grace Groner) that I wrote about in Chapter 2. Of these three individuals, particular praise must be given to Andrew Hallam, who remains one of my favourite investment writers and a key influence on my investing philosophy. Check out episode twenty-eight of *The Sloth Investor* podcast for my interview with him.

I would also like to thank Jason Prohaska, the co-host of *The Sloth Investor* podcast. During the many episodes that we have recorded together, Jason has enabled me to test, refine and extend many of my ideas concerning investing. Thanks, Jason!

I would also like to take this opportunity to thank my father-in-law, John. I've participated in many hours of spirited discussions with John concerning investing and, given that I come from a family of 'non-investors' (I know… perish the thought), it is undoubtedly the case that John's wise guidance in my early years of investing set me on the path to becoming the Sloth Investor.

During numerous occasions while writing this book, I thought about my late mother. Mum encouraged me to be curious and my appetite to learn can be attributed to the healthy reading habit that she instilled within me from a young age. Thank you, Mum, for encouraging me to read and for setting such a good example to me through your own love of reading. I guess the apple doesn't fall far from the tree (now it just contains a sloth).

Writing *The Sloth Investor* was a double helix of love and labour. This book wouldn't exist without the unrelenting encouragement of my wife, Justine (Mrs Sloth). I would like to extend my deep gratitude to her for her patience while reading early drafts of this book and for providing me with suggestions. Thanks, Justine!

Finally, thank you to Leo and Keira (my mini sloth investors). May you grow up to be fully fledged sloth investors!

About the Author

The Sloth Investor (or 'Mr Sloth') is R P Stevens, the host of *The Sloth Investor* podcast. His mission is to simplify investing for all, enabling people to understand the wisdom of an inactive approach to investing. Born in the UK, he now lives in Hong Kong with his wife ('Mrs Sloth') and their two children.

THANKS FOR READING!

Thanks for reading my book!

I hope you enjoyed reading *The Sloth Investor* and that it provided you with value.

It would mean a great deal to me if you left an Amazon review. I appreciate and value all of your feedback.

Simply find this book on Amazon, scroll to the reviews section, and click 'Write a customer review'. I love hearing what you have to say.

In addition to this book and my YouTube channel, I also provide a series of in-person and online investment literacy workshops about how beginner investors can 'invest like a sloth'.

I can be contacted at mrsloth@slothinvestor.com

Thanks so much!

R P Stevens
aka 'The Sloth Investor'

This book is printed on paper from sustainable sources managed under the Forest Stewardship Council (FSC) scheme.

It has been printed in the UK to reduce transportation miles and their impact upon the environment.

For every new title that Troubador publishes, we plant a tree to offset CO_2, partnering with the More Trees scheme.

For more about how Troubador offsets its environmental impact, see www.troubador.co.uk/sustainability-and-community